DECONSTRUCTING
DEPTH *of*
KNOWLEDGE

A Method and Model for Deeper Teaching and Learning

ERIK M. FRANCIS

FOREWORD BY KARIN HESS

Solution Tree | Press

a division of
Solution Tree

Norman Webb developed Webb's Depth-of-Knowledge definitions in 1997 as a tool to analyze alignment between curriculum standards and assessments. At the time he was a Senior Research Scientist for the Wisconsin Center for Education Research and was funded in part by the National Science Foundation (cooperative agreement No. RED-9452971). The DOK definitions describe levels or categories of cognitive complexity. They are not intended to represent progressions in learning or instructional levels. The Wisconsin Center for Education Products and Services (WCEPS) manages WebbAlign™, the trademark for Webb's DOK™. Updated definitions and supporting materials can be found at www.webbalign.org.

555 North Morton Street
Bloomington, IN 47404
800.733.6786 (toll free) / 812.336.7700
FAX: 812.336.7790

email: info@SolutionTree.com
SolutionTree.com

Visit **go.SolutionTree.com/instruction** to download the free reproducibles in this book.

Printed in the United States of America

Library of Congress Cataloging-in-Publication Data

Names: Francis, Erik M., author.
Title: Deconstructing depth of knowledge : a method and model for deeper
    teaching and learning / Erik M. Francis.
Description: Bloomington, IN : Solution Tree Press, [2021] | Includes
    bibliographical references and index.
Identifiers: LCCN 2021040147 (print) | LCCN 2021040148 (ebook) | ISBN
    9781951075156 (paperback) | ISBN 9781951075163 (ebook)
Subjects: LCSH: Webb, Norman. | Cognitive learning--United States. |
    Knowledge, Theory of, in children--United States. | Effective
    teaching--United States. | Teaching--Methodology. |
    Education--Standards--United States.
Classification: LCC LB1062 .F72 2021 (print) | LCC LB1062 (ebook) | DDC
    370.15/230973--dc23/eng/20211027
LC record available at https://lccn.loc.gov/2021040147
LC ebook record available at https://lccn.loc.gov/2021040148

Solution Tree
Jeffrey C. Jones, CEO
Edmund M. Ackerman, President

Solution Tree Press

President and Publisher: Douglas M. Rife
Associate Publisher: Sarah Payne-Mills
Managing Production Editor: Kendra Slayton
Editorial Director: Todd Brakke
Art Director: Rian Anderson
Copy Chief: Jessi Finn
Production Editor: Alissa Voss
Content Development Specialist: Amy Rubenstein
Copy Editor: Kate St. Ives
Proofreader: Elisabeth Abrams
Text and Cover Designer: Kelsey Hergül
Editorial Assistants: Sarah Ludwig and Elijah Oates

ACKNOWLEDGMENTS

To my wife, Susie Francis—thank you for your love, support, and patience, especially as I constantly bounced ideas off you and asked your thoughts on how students in grades K–3 might demonstrate or experience Depth of Knowledge even as you spent long days teaching first graders remotely on hybrid and virtual platforms. You helped me keep things in perspective and keep a positive outlook. You kept reminding me to focus on what people will need in the future rather than perseverate on the present. You also made sure I took breaks to take a ride on the Peloton, go in the garage and lift weights, or binge-watch a TV series you discovered. This all helped ease my mind and shape the ideas and strategies in this book.

To my daughters, Madison and Avery—you both are the best daughters a dad could hope to have. The pandemic was neither easy nor fair for either of you—Madison, with you finishing, and Avery, with you beginning your high school career during this pandemic. However, you both survived and thrived through this experience, and your resilience both impressed and inspired me. Take what you learned through your education and experience, and use your gifts and talents to do great things. I am proud of both of you and love you very much.

Thanks to my mom, Julia Francis, for always being there to listen whenever I was brainstorming or having writer's block. You always made me feel like every idea I came up with was great, and you always reminded me to go to the Shire when I felt frustrated or stressed. Also, thank you to my mother, Wendy Latman, for your encouragement and support in my endeavors professionally and personally.

I also want to thank Amy Rubenstein, my content editor at Solution Tree, for helping me craft this book and make Depth of Knowledge clear and comprehensible. You guided me to recognize what should be said, realize what changes must be made, and remember that "You can always save this for another book." Also, thanks to Alissa Voss, my editor from the land down under, for making sure this book was grammatically correct and clear and encouraging me to elaborate further on the ideas and strategies featured in this book. Both of you provided valuable feedback and suggestions that made this book better and stronger.

I also want to express my appreciation to Solution Tree for publishing this book. Claudia Wheatley—thank you for introducing me to Solution Tree, for appreciating my ideas and my work, and for believing I have what it takes to be a Solution Tree author. Douglas Rife—thank you not only for agreeing to publish this book but also making me feel like I was a valued member of the Solution Tree team even before I signed the contract. Jeff Jones—thank you for always taking the time to talk whenever we crossed paths and asking, "So when are you going to write that book for us?" Well, here it is, and I am honored to be a Solution Tree author.

Authoring this book also provided me the opportunity to solidify and strengthen relationships with several people professionally and personally. People like Tom Hierck, who kept encouraging me to think critically about how education will change, to think creatively about how to lead and facilitate that change, and "to keep my focus/energy on the positive and don't get sucked down the black hole" (a quote from a text you sent me on July 20, 2021). Then there's Paula Maeker, who always took time to listen and brainstorm, confirmed or challenged my knowledge and thinking, and reminded me it's about how we do and use "the work" to benefit and serve others. Thank you both for being tremendous advocates and supporters.

I also want to thank the following colleagues and friends who shared their expertise with me and inspired me to think extensively how Depth of Knowledge could complement and support their work: Dr. Katherine McKnight, Dr. Richard Cash, Dr. Jaime Castellano, Dr. Joseph Renzulli, Rick Wormeli, Sara Christopherson from WebbAlign, and, most especially, Dr. Norman L. Webb and Dr. Karin Hess. I appreciate all you have taught me, your collegiality, and your support.

I want to thank the following school leaders who provided me the opportunity to train their teachers on Depth of Knowledge: Rhonda Newton from All Aboard Charter School in Phoenix, Arizona; Carolyn Sawyer from Champion Schools in Phoenix, Arizona; Christopher Hallett, executive director of the Northern Maine Education Collaborative (NMEC); Diana Diaz-Harrison and Lisa Long from Arizona Autism Charter School in Phoenix, Arizona; Kathy Scott from Nogales Unified School District in Nogales, Arizona; Rose Mogus, Rob Housel, and Kristi McDermitt from Summit Academy Canton Elementary in Canton, Ohio; and Koshu Lulla, director of Tele-Temps PTE Limited and Secretariat of Singapore ASCD in Singapore and Malaysia.

Working with your educators helped me create and shape the ideas and strategies addressed in this book.

I also want to thank my good friends who were always there to listen and provide their input and support: Gary Horowitz, Dr. Rick Jetter, Rebecca Coda, LaVonna Roth, Dr. Holly Couturier, Lynne Henwood, Greg Wolcott, Tee Lambert, Michael Brien Lane, and Brad Astrowsky.

Finally, I dedicate this book to my father, my best friend, and my hero, Fred Francis, who instilled in me the importance and value of lifelong learning and taught me how to learn and live life at all the DOK levels—especially the deeper ones that engage to understand and use our knowledge and skills to prove it or encourage us to go for it.

Solution Tree Press would like to thank the following reviewers:

Larissa Bailey
Second-Grade Teacher
Pleasant Valley School District
Bettendorf, Iowa

Betsy Furr
Curriculum Specialist
Watauga County Schools
Boone, North Carolina

Jenn Basner
Fifth-Grade Teacher
Berlin Community School
Berlin, New Jersey

Kristin Grinager
High School Curriculum Coordinator
Sioux Falls School District
Sioux Falls, South Dakota

Kirsten Britt
English Teacher
Norwalk Middle School
Norwalk, Iowa

Kendra Hanzlik
Instructional Coach
Prairie Hill Elementary School
Cedar Rapids, Iowa

Paul Cancellieri
Science Teacher
Rolesville Middle School
Rolesville, North Carolina

Kelly Hilliard
Math Teacher
McQueen High School
Reno, Nevada

Hallie Edgerly
Science Teacher
Adel DeSoto Minburn Middle School
Adel, Iowa

Amy Kochensparger
Science Teacher
Eaton High School
Eaton, Ohio

Jenna Fanshier
Sixth-Grade Teacher
Hesston Middle School
Hesston, Kansas

Erin Kowalik
Biology Teacher
James Bowie High School
Austin, Texas

Megan Nicholson
Fourth-Grade Teacher
Franklin Elementary School
Logansport, Indiana

Tara Reed
Fourth-Grade Teacher
Hawk Elementary School
Corinth, Texas

Bo Ryan
Principal
Greater Hartford Academy of the Arts
  Middle School
Hartford, Connecticut

Visit **go.SolutionTree.com/instruction** to
download the free reproducibles in this book.

TABLE OF CONTENTS

Reproducible pages are in italics.

PART ONE

UNDERSTANDING DEPTH OF KNOWLEDGE · 7

PART II

USING DEPTH OF KNOWLEDGE   83

Praise for

Deconstructing Depth of Knowledge:

A Method and Model for Deeper Teaching and Learning

"In *Deconstructing Depth of Knowledge*, Eric M. Francis masterfully explains the often-misunderstood Depth of Knowledge framework. He walks you through the myths and misperceptions of the model and ultimately gives you the tools to apply it with fidelity in your classroom. This book should be on every educator's desk and should be the guide to deepening understanding for all students."

—Richard M. Cash
Educator, Author, and Consultant, nRich Educational Consulting, Inc.

"Forget the wheel! *Deconstructing Depth of Knowledge* takes what was once a mysterious and elusive concept and makes it practical, approachable, and doable. This resource explicitly examines what Depth of Knowledge is and is not and moves beyond theory and misconceptions to create a clear framework of implementation for every educator, at every content, and at any level. Erik Francis has not only aligned his content to current research and pedagogy, but he also maintains the message throughout this book that all students can learn at high levels, and it is the work of educators that achieves this goal. Through this book, he actually shows us how."

—Paula Maeker
Educator, Consultant, and Advocate for Learner-Centered Education

"Take a look at this book, and you'll see why Global Gurus identifies Erik M. Francis as one of the world's Top 30 Education Professionals 2021. *Deconstructing Depth of Knowledge* presents teachers and administrators with a blueprint for the successful application of Depth of Knowledge with any student population. The tables, figures, and templates throughout the book help explain why it is such a valuable resource, and the multiple examples make the concepts easy to follow. The how-to nature of the book also makes it appropriate for veteran, mid-career, and novice teachers alike. Readers can turn to any chapter and immediately find an abundance of information, examples, and direction for using the principles for deeper teaching and learning with students. This book is a must-have for educators at any level of teaching."

—Jaime Castellano
Educator, Author, and Professor, Florida Atlantic University

ABOUT THE AUTHOR

 **Erik M. Francis, MEd, MS,** is an international author and presenter who specializes in teaching and learning for cognitive rigor. An educator for over twenty-five years, Erik has experience as a classroom teacher, a site administrator, an education program specialist with a state education agency, and a professional development trainer. Erik is the owner of Maverik Education, providing professional development and consultation on developing and delivering authentic, student-centered educational experiences. His areas of expertise include Depth of Knowledge (DOK), questioning and inquiry, authentic learning, differentiated instruction, personalized learning, and talent development.

Erik has conducted professional development trainings and workshops at K–12 schools, colleges, and universities throughout the United States and internationally. His academic seminars have been featured at national, state, and regional education conferences hosted by organizations such as ASCD, Learning Forward, the College Board, the Association for Middle Level Education, the National Association for Gifted Children, the National Teacher Center, and the Southern Regional Education Board. He has extensive experience working with students who are academically at risk, gifted and talented (GT) students, English learners (EL or ELL), and exceptional students with special needs.

Erik is the author of *Now That's a Good Question! How to Promote Cognitive Rigor Through Classroom Questioning.* He was also ranked as one of the world's Top Thirty Education Professionals for 2019 by the research organization Global Gurus.

Erik received a master's degree in education leadership from Northern Arizona University and a master of science in television, radio, and film production and management from the S. I. Newhouse School of Public Communications at Syracuse University. He also holds a bachelor of arts in rhetoric and communication and English from the State University of New York at Albany.

To learn more about Erik's work, visit Maverik Education (https://maverikeducation .com), or follow @Maverikedu12 on Twitter.

To book Erik M. Francis for professional development, contact pd@SolutionTree .com.

FOREWORD

by Karin Hess

Author of the Hess Cognitive Rigor Matrix, *A Local Assessment Toolkit to Promote Deeper Learning, Deeper Competency-Based Learning*, and *Rigor by Design*

Like many teachers, I was introduced to Bloom's taxonomy as the "gold standard" for designing higher-order thinking into my lessons. It was two decades later that I came across Norman Webb's alignment study white papers in the 1990s and began to use Depth of Knowledge (DOK) in my work with states that were developing state standards and state assessments. Many teachers on state committees involved with this work asked how they could use DOK in planning their own instruction. Because of the positive feedback I was hearing, in 2008, I submitted my first article for publication describing how DOK could be used to plan rigorous instruction and assessment. The rejection letter I received stated that this idea would not be useful to most educators. I'm glad I didn't listen to that editor because today DOK is used in countries around the world by test developers, curriculum developers, and mostly by classroom teachers to establish a range of engagement with content to be taught and assessed. As with the widespread use of many educational frameworks, however, there are often misconceptions and missteps in the application of DOK—the most common one being that a verb can indicate the intended DOK level of a question or a task.

Erik M. Francis's book immediately launches into a counterargument to dispel this misconception and oversimplification of DOK related to verbs and "the verb wheel" that I still see in the hands of teachers who attend my workshops. He first provides an historical context for his claim, citing the work of prominent educators who have also written extensively about rigor and why verbs alone cannot tell the whole story. Then he posits a broader view of DOK, stating, "I believe teaching and learning for Depth of Knowledge is not only an academic method or model that promotes rigorous instruction, learning, or assessment. Depth of Knowledge also fosters and promotes a growth mindset for teaching and learning." The introduction ends with a challenge to readers to adopt a new mindset based on Four Tenets of Depth of Knowledge. Collaborative discussions based on these Four Tenets can be a way to build a foundation for deconstructing DOK with colleagues in order to develop a shared understanding of how the strategies presented throughout the book could result in a new mindset about the use of DOK.

Part 1 of the book then begins the DOK deconstruction, weaving in and drawing upon perspectives of many well-respected educators to address other common misconceptions—the difference between difficulty and cognitive demand and the misunderstanding that DOK is just another taxonomy, like Bloom's taxonomy. This discussion builds a rationale for the development and use of the author's DOK blocks—a visual model that depicts the nominative nature and structure of DOK levels as building blocks. Each DOK block can be used to identify the intended DOK level a specific academic standard, learning activity, or assessment task demands. Especially useful to teachers are the content-specific examples for using the blocks in lesson planning, found throughout the rest of the book. Francis ends part 1 by introducing a way for educators to think about how DOK levels might intersect with conceptualizing a multitiered system of supports (MTSS) for delivering instruction, responding to intervention (RTI), and extending student learning for gifted learners, an idea explored in depth in chapter 4. The ideas presented in chapter 4 will be new to most educators and are sure to spark ongoing discussions about meeting individual student needs while setting high expectations for every learner.

Part 2 of the book provides specific strategies and numerous content examples showing how to consider the relationship among types of thinking (cognitive actions) and Depth of Knowledge broken down into three subareas: (1) the instructional focus, (2) the instructional purpose, and (3) DOK skills. This planning approach offers multiple entry points to educators who have used other methods to unpack standards that might not have included a useful lens for applying DOK. Most helpful are the planning tools with content examples showing how the same verb (cognitive action) might be used at different DOK levels, bringing the ideas presented in the introduction full circle—it's not just about the verb!

Each chapter ends with both a summary of key ideas presented and questions for professional learning communities (PLCs) to reflect on, discuss, and explore together. There are no "right answers" to these questions; however, as schools move toward developing a new mindset about using DOK, the questions may help to reframe some current practices and beliefs about rigorous teaching and learning that all students can benefit from.

INTRODUCTION

The only possible use of the chart I can see is
if someone took a verb and asked how it could
be placed in each of the four sectors.

—NORMAN L. WEBB

It seemed to come out of nowhere, this academic framework with the three-letter acronym—DOK, Depth of Knowledge. It proliferated in the world of education as a new focus and goal for schools, staff, and students in the 21st century. However, it was first introduced in the late 1990s as a criterion for alignment studies, not as an academic concept for teaching and learning.

It seemed to be a new instructional approach, a practice for developing and delivering rigorous teaching and learning experiences. It's actually a measure of cognitive rigor, not an instructional method.

It seemed to be another taxonomy that classifies and measures the complexity of types of thinking. However, Depth of Knowledge is not a taxonomy. It's also not about the cognitive action students must perform as indicated by "the verb." Instead, it considers the complexity of the content knowledge students must learn, and the depth and extent—or context— in which students must understand and use their learning.

Many academics, authors, bloggers, educators, presenters, and professional development providers, including me, have attempted to explain what Depth of Knowledge is—and what it is *not*. If you google *Depth of Knowledge*, *DOK*, or *Webb's DOK*, you'll return over 750 million hits, depending on the day. Some sources reference the research of Norman L. Webb (1997, 1999), who developed Depth of Knowledge as a criterion for judging the alignment between academic standards and assessments, while others are more aligned to the work of Karin Hess, who superimposed Webb's Depth of Knowledge levels with Bloom's revised taxonomy to measure the cognitive rigor of academic standards and the activities, items, and tasks that address and assess them (with Carlock, Jones, & Walkup, 2009a, 2009b). Most literature, presentations, and trainings on Depth of Knowledge feature the Depth of

Knowledge wheel (viewable online at www.state.nj.us/education/AchieveNJ/teacher /DOKWheelAndDOKRigorChartAndChecklist.pdf).

The DOK wheel is one of many visuals that attempts to represent Depth of Knowledge graphically. The wheel is the most widely known because it was included in the training materials for the Common Core State Standards. Participants in the CCSS trainings were taught how to use the DOK wheel to determine the cognitive demand of an academic standard, activity, or assessment. The DOK level depended on which spoke featured the verb from the academic standard, activity, or assessment item's learning intention or objective.

Unfortunately, the DOK wheel is inaccurate.

Yes, you read that right. The DOK wheel, despite its widespread distribution and use, depicts Depth of Knowledge—specifically, Webb's Depth of Knowledge levels—incorrectly.

You're probably wondering how this could be. The DOK wheel is everywhere! It's provided in trainings on teaching and testing college and career readiness standards. It's posted on state, county, regional, and local education agency websites. It's featured in numerous articles, blogs, presentations, and webinars. It's one of the first graphics that comes up in a Google search. The poster featuring the DOK wheel (see www.state .nj.us/education/AchieveNJ/teacher/DOKWheelAndDOKRigorChartAndChecklist .pdf) even cites Webb, and others, as the creators.

However, Webb did not create the DOK wheel. In fact, he considers it "misleading and has always discouraged its use" (Walkup, 2013). If you contact Webb or his organization, WebbAlign, you will be informed that Webb "did not create the DOK wheel, does not endorse it, and does not believe it represents the four dimensions" (Blackburn & Witzel, 2018, pp. 40–41).

So, if it wasn't Webb, who created the DOK wheel? No one knows for sure. According to Dr. Webb, he first encountered the DOK wheel in the mid-2000s when he facilitated alignment studies of Florida's state standards and assessment (N. Webb, personal communication, July 5, 2018). He also reiterated he did not create the DOK wheel and tells people not to use it. It's presumed that an educator from Florida uploaded the DOK wheel to the internet to help schools and staff understand the concept better. Unfortunately, it caused and created more confusion.

Hess (2018) speculates the DOK wheel may have been derived from a Bloom's taxonomy wheel featured in *Growing Up Gifted* by Barbara Clark (1983). The only difference is that Clark's HOT wheel lists cognitive action verbs in five spokes, and the DOK wheel features them in four. The DOK wheel also implies that a learning experience must start at DOK level 1 or DOK level 2 before students can demonstrate their learning at a DOK level 3 or DOK level 4.

The biggest problem with the DOK wheel is it implies the Depth of Knowledge demanded by an academic standard, activity, or assessment depends on the type of thinking students will demonstrate as defined by "the verb" that introduces its learning intention, objective, or target. That's why so many educators misinterpret Depth of Knowledge and Webb's DOK levels another way to "do Bloom's."

Then, you may ask, what exactly is Depth of Knowledge? This book articulates my ideas of what Depth of Knowledge is and how the DOK levels can serve as a method and model that inform how teaching and learning experiences can be developed, delivered, and deepened. It takes inspiration from Norman Webb's research with alignment studies and Karin Hess's concept of cognitive rigor. It provides a process not only to determine the demand of academic standards, activities, and assessments but also to drive decisions regarding how to address, assess, assist, and augment students' ability to achieve and surpass grade-level or curricular goals and expectations. Most importantly, it explores and explains with examples and evidence how educators and practitioners can plan and provide engaging teaching and learning experiences that are academically rigorous, socially and emotionally supportive, and student responsive.

The Four Tenets of DOK

Depth of Knowledge has become a focus and priority for schools, staff, and systems around the world. However, over the years, DOK and Webb's DOK levels have been interpreted and re-interpreted in many ways, some closer to the intent than others. To honor, respect, and distinguish the great work of both Norman Webb and Karin Hess with Depth of Knowledge, I want to make it very clear that this is my interpretation of DOK and the DOK levels. Although this book draws inspiration and influence from their work, like DOK itself, this book provides a different and deeper perspective of Depth of Knowledge and how the DOK levels have been viewed and used.

I believe teaching and learning for Depth of Knowledge is not only an academic method or model that promotes rigorous instruction, learning, or assessment. It also fosters and promotes a growth mindset for teaching and learning. Educators can use the DOK levels to state or specify learning goals and expectations. We could also use the DOK levels to show and share with students how they could achieve and surpass both proficiency and personal goals and expectations.

To adopt this mindset effectively, all staff and students should accept and agree to what I call the Four Tenets of Depth of Knowledge.

1. Teaching and testing for DOK address and assess student learning over a range of DOK levels leading to the Depth of Knowledge demanded by a learning intention or its most cognitively demanding objective.

2. Teaching and learning for DOK tier to and build on the strength of the students so they can achieve and surpass the level of Depth of Knowledge demanded by a learning intention or its most cognitively demanding objective.

3. All students are expected and encouraged to understand and use their learning at and beyond the level of Depth of Knowledge demanded by a learning intention or its most cognitively demanding objective.

4. All students will be guided and supported to develop, demonstrate, and deepen their learning over a range of DOK levels leading to and beyond a learning intention or its most cognitively demanding objective.

The tenets show how teaching and learning for Depth of Knowledge are both a practice and a philosophy. If our students are to understand and use their learning at different and deeper DOK levels successfully, then we educators must agree and adhere to these beliefs and principles. Subsequent chapters of this book explain how to apply these tenets and use the DOK blocks to develop and deliver teaching and learning experiences that address and assess Depth of Knowledge.

What's in This Book

This book is divided into two parts. Part I, chapters 1–4, presents theoretical information deconstructing Depth of Knowledge to ensure readers correctly understand the model and its associated levels. Chapter 1 discusses what Depth of Knowledge really is: a different and deeper way of looking at teaching and learning. It explains how Depth of Knowledge involves looking beyond the verb to confirm what students are learning and how deeply they must demonstrate their learning. It distinguishes Webb's DOK levels from other cognitive frameworks educators use to plan and provide instruction and assessment. It also introduces the DOK blocks, a graphic I created that not only indicates the demand of the standard but also informs the delivery and intensity of the instruction students should experience. Chapters 2 through 4 focus on how Depth of Knowledge is a method, model, and mindset for teaching and learning. Chapter 2 describes the instructional focus and purpose of teaching and learning at each DOK level. Chapter 3 explains how Depth of Knowledge strengthens and supports standards, assessment, instruction, learning, and the curriculum. Chapter 4 shows how teachers can use the DOK levels as a multitiered system of supports

(MTSS) for delivering instruction, responding to intervention, and extending student learning. Each of these chapters concludes with reflection questions about *understanding* Depth of Knowledge. These questions engage you to think strategically how you could apply Depth of Knowledge to your area or role in education.

Part II, chapters 5–9, focuses on applying the Depth of Knowledge model, explaining how to plan and provide DOK teaching and learning experiences. Chapter 5 shows how to deconstruct the learning intention of an academic standard to identify its instructional focus and inform its instructional purpose. Chapter 6 discusses how to designate the DOK level a task demands by examining the mental processing students must perform or responses they must provide. Chapter 7 shows how to reconstruct the learning intention of academic standards into DOK learning targets for units and lessons and DOK success criteria for activities and assessments. Chapter 8 explains how to ask good questions that will prompt students to reflect and respond at different and deeper DOK levels. Finally, chapter 9 compares the goals and expectations of the DOK levels to several types of television shows and genres. It also illustrates how teachers can simulate the format of such TV shows and genres to create DOK teaching and learning experiences for students at each of the DOK levels. The chapters in part II end with professional development activities that encourage you to think extensively about *using* Depth of Knowledge—specifically, how you could develop and deliver teaching and learning experiences that will demand students understand and use their learning at different and deeper DOK levels.

Who This Book Is For

My goal and purpose for this book are to explain how K–12 educators could use Depth of Knowledge and the DOK levels constructively and creatively to develop and deliver deeper teaching and learning experiences. I consider this book my DOK 4 because it encouraged me to think extensively and to explore and explain with examples and evidence how Depth of Knowledge and the DOK levels could be used as a method and model to strengthen and support student performance and teacher effectiveness.

If you're a classroom teacher or instructional specialist, you'll recognize the goal and expectations of teaching and learning at each DOK level. You will also realize how you can use the DOK levels to plan and provide educational experiences that are academically rigorous, socially and emotionally supportive, and student responsive.

If you're an instructional leader or coach, you will recognize what teaching and learning for Depth of Knowledge look like. You will also realize how you might use the DOK levels as a resource to guide and support your staff by differentiating and intensifying their instruction based on the demands of the standards and the strengths and successes of the students.

If you're an academic standards or assessment specialist for a national, state, or local education agency, you will recognize how Depth of Knowledge is a criterion for alignment studies and realize how to use the DOK levels to categorize and compare the cognitive demand of grade-level expectations and assessments and determine their degree of alignment—or what Webb (1999) calls *DOK consistency*.

If you're a curriculum or assessment designer, you'll recognize how Depth of Knowledge is defined by the demands of the task, the mental processing skills students must perform, and the responses students must provide. You will also realize how you can use the DOK levels to create activities, items, and tasks that will require that students develop, demonstrate, and deepen their knowledge and skills.

However, as the *G.I. Joe* cartoon from the 1980s said in its public service announcements featured at the end of each episode, "Knowing is half the battle!" Keep that in mind as you read this book and consider how truly understanding and using Depth of Knowledge can increase and improve the performance and potential of your students, staff, school, or system.

PART ONE

UNDERSTANDING
DEPTH *of* KNOWLEDGE

CHAPTER ONE

What Exactly Is Depth of Knowledge?

Suppose you are planning a unit or lesson in the content area for your grade level. You choose the academic standard that will be addressed and assessed. You then unpack, or unwrap, the standard to determine what students must know and be able to do. According to Larry Ainsworth (2003), the "important nouns and noun phrases" identify the key concepts and content students will learn, and the verbs indicate the skills students will develop. Both noun and verb state what Robert Mager (1997) calls the *performance*, "what a learner is expected to be able to do to be considered competent" (p. 46).

You check where the verb—or cognitive action—is listed in a learning taxonomy that classifies types of thinking based on complexity. Perhaps you'll use the Taxonomy of Educational Objectives developed by Benjamin Bloom (1956) or the revised version by Lorin Anderson and David Krathwohl (2001). Perhaps you'll consult John Biggs's Structure of Observed Learning Outcome—or SOLO—taxonomy (Biggs & Collis, 1982), the Six Facets of Understanding by Grant Wiggins and Jay McTighe (2005), Art Costa's Levels of Questioning (Costa & Kallick, 2008), Robert Marzano's Taxonomy of Educational Objectives (Marzano & Kendall, 2007), or L. Dee Fink's (2013) Taxonomy of Significant Learning. In all these taxonomies, the higher the level at which the verb is categorized, the more complex the learning intention of the standard according to the logic of the taxonomy. The levels of these taxonomies also build on each other or *scaffold*, intimating that teaching and testing must address and assess student learning at a lower level of thinking before they can demonstrate higher-level thinking.

However, what exactly is the content knowledge that students must learn? Also, how deeply do the conditions and criteria—or context—demand students understand and use their knowledge and thinking or learning?

To verify this, we need to look at all the words and phrases that follow the initial cognitive action verb of the standard's learning intention or individual objectives. Those words and phrases state what exactly and specify how deeply students must understand and use their learning to answer questions, address problems, accomplish tasks, or analyze texts and topics. They also determine the level of cognitive demand—or Depth of Knowledge—according to the DOK levels developed by Dr. Norman Webb (1999).

Yet, why does determining the Depth of Knowledge demanded involve looking beyond the verb of a learning intention, objective, or target? How is Depth of Knowledge based on demand, not difficulty? How do the DOK levels designate four different and deeper ways—or contexts—in which students can understand and use learning? How can Depth of Knowledge and the DOK levels be used to determine the degree of alignment between academic standards, lessons, and assessments; to measure the cognitive rigor of a curricular activity or test item; and as a method, model, and mindset for teaching and learning?

To answer these questions, this chapter first defines Depth of Knowledge and explains why DOK requires looking beyond the type and complexity of thinking—or beyond *the verb*— students will demonstrate. It highlights that, while teaching for Depth of Knowledge is demanding, it isn't difficult. Next, it provides an explanation of what the DOK levels are and why they are not a taxonomy. Finally, it introduces a new visual—the DOK blocks—that not only depicts the nominative nature and structure of the DOK levels but also describes how to develop and deliver teaching and learning experiences at different DOK levels.

Depth of Knowledge Deconstructed

Depth of Knowledge is a different and deeper way of looking at academic standards, activities, and assessments. It is a resource and a tool "that allows educators to communicate effectively, consistently, and efficiently about the content complexity of standards, learning objectives, tasks, prompts, questions, etc." (Webb, 2019, p. 1). It also provides a clear and coherent language system both educators and students could understand and use to consider, confirm, and communicate the cognitive demand of academic standards, curricular activities, and assessment items.

The level of Depth of Knowledge demanded can vary based on several factors, including the following (Webb, 1997).

- The complexity and number of ideas and information students must know and apply
- The prerequisite knowledge students must acquire and possess to grasp ideas
- The depth of reasoning required
- The ability to transfer learning in different contexts
- The number and variety of representations employed
- The mental effort required and sustained to answer a question, address a problem, accomplish a task, or analyze a text or topic

To determine the Depth of Knowledge an academic standard, activity, or assessment demands, we need to check and clarify the following.

- What is the complexity of the content knowledge students must learn?
- How deeply does the context demand students understand and use their knowledge and thinking or learning?

The response to these questions will determine the cognitive demand of the following.

- The activity, item, or task students must complete (DOK task)
- The specific mental processing students must perform (DOK skill)
- The response students must provide (DOK response)

I have developed this process to determine the level of Depth of Knowledge demanded by academic standards, activities, and assessments. I will elaborate on the process further in the second part of this book (page 83). However, before we engage in this process, we need to understand what exactly Depth of Knowledge is and how it has evolved from a criterion for alignment studies to a measure of cognitive rigor to a method and model that inform ideas about teaching and learning. No matter how it is presented or portrayed, understanding and using Depth of Knowledge as both an academic concept and framework require comprehension of four essential issues.

1. Depth of Knowledge requires looking beyond the verb of a learning intention or objective.
2. Depth of Knowledge is demanding, not difficult.
3. Webb's DOK levels are not a taxonomy.
4. The DOK levels categorize and describe the ways students can understand and use their learning.

The following sections will elaborate on these points.

Depth of Knowledge Requires Looking Beyond the Verb

A common misconception about Depth of Knowledge is that it refers to the type of thinking students will demonstrate. This is due to inaccurate graphics such as the DOK wheel, which suggest the Depth of Knowledge demanded can be increased or decreased by using or changing the verb.

What's wrong with the verb? Absolutely nothing—if you're teaching and testing for different levels of thinking. However, verbs do not describe the complexity of content knowledge students will learn. They also do not detail the depth and extent to which students must demonstrate their learning in a certain context. Instead, they indicate the type of thinking—or cognitive action—students will demonstrate to answer a question, solve a problem, or complete a task. For example:

- "Explain why addition and subtraction strategies work, using place value and the properties of operations." (CCSS.Math-Content.2.NBT.B.9; National Governors Association Center for Best Practices & Council of Chief State School Officers [NGA & CCSSO], 2010a)

- "Explain how the use of text structure contributes to the author's purpose." (TEKS.ELA.4.10.B; Texas Education Agency, 2011)

- "Explain the difference between solids, liquids, and gases in terms of density, using the particle theory of matter." (Ontario.Science.8.ULS.3.4; Ontario Ministry of Education, 2007)

- "Explain how the perspectives of people in the present shape interpretations of the past." (C3.D2.His.7.9–12; National Council for the Social Studies, 2013)

- "Explain the differences and similarities between the word structures (derivation, prefixes, suffixes, etc.) in the target language and their own." (AERO.4.1.G5.c; Project AERO, 2018)

- "Explain how the method of display, the location, and the experience of an artwork influence how it is perceived." (NCAS.VA:Re.7.1.7a; State Education Agency Directors of Arts Education, 2014)

- "Explain how responses to music are informed by the structure, the use of the elements of music, and context (such as social and cultural)." (NCAS.MU:Re7.2.4; State Education Agency Directors of Arts Education, 2014)

- "Explain how body systems interact with one another during physical activity." (S3.M14.8; SHAPE America, 2013)

- "Explain the difference between civil law and criminal law."
  (ACHCK064; Department of Education, Skills, and Employment, 2015)

- "Explain the reasons for the rise and decline of early Singapore
  (Temasek) as a port-of-call across time." (Singapore MOE.History.Lower
  Secondary.1.2; Ministry of Education Singapore, 2021)

Each of these grade-level academic standards expects students to *explain*. That's the type of thinking—or cognitive action—students will demonstrate or perform. However, what exactly is the complexity of the content knowledge students must explain? Also, how deeply must students explain the content knowledge? The verb neither states nor specifies this.

Cognitive action verbs are also abstract and have multiple meanings, making their level of demand difficult to define. For example, when students are expected to *explain*, it could mean they are required to provide details, information, or a description; challenged to make clear or put in their own words; engaged to account for or give reasons; encouraged to make connections or show relationships; or all of the above! Webb (1999) also points out that verbs "could be interpreted in different ways, making it more difficult . . . to designate a specific depth-of-knowledge level" (p. 23). Further clarification is needed to determine the depth and extent to which a learning intention or target demands students demonstrate their learning.

We could check where the cognitive action verb is categorized in a learning taxonomy. That's how we have traditionally judged the complexity and quality of an academic standard, activity, or assessment. However, the problem with learning taxonomies is that "many verbs appear at multiple levels and do not clearly articulate the intended complexity implied by the taxonomy" (Hess et al., 2009a, p. 2). For example, iterations and versions of Bloom's revised taxonomy list "to explain" under the cognitive levels *Remember, Understand, Analyze*, and *Evaluate* (Anderson & Krathwohl, 2001). Marzano's Taxonomy of Educational Objectives (Marzano & Kendall, 2007) features "to explain" in different forms under its levels *Comprehension* and *Analysis*. The level of complexity of the verb can also depend on the taxonomy being used. For example, in Bloom's revised taxonomy, explaining is the highest subcategory under the level *Understand*. However, explanation is the base level of understanding students can demonstrate according to Wiggins and McTighe's (2005) Six Facets of Understanding. The SOLO taxonomy (Biggs & Collis, 1982) lists "to explain" under *Relational*, the third of its four levels.

Cognitive action verbs also have what Anderson and Krathwohl (2001) call *alternative names*. These verbs attempt to specify the mental processing skills students must perform. However, some of these verbs are just as broad or vague. They can also vary in their level of complexity. For example, in their analysis of the vocabulary used in college and career readiness standards, Robert J. Marzano and Julia A. Simms (2013; Marzano, Rogers, & Simms, 2015) identified eighteen cognitive action verbs synonymous with explaining. These verbs include accounting, answering, articulating, clarifying, conveying, describing, expressing, guiding, indicating, narrating, summarizing, and synthesizing—all cognitive actions that differ in their level of complexity. Even if we replaced "to explain" with one of these alternative names, the verb alone would not identify the complexity of the content knowledge students must learn or the context in which they must demonstrate their learning.

The specific mental-processing skill students must perform also depends on the kind of content knowledge students are studying. For example, explaining something in a subject that is highly detail-oriented or text-dependent could demand students to recall or use information as examples or evidence along with basic, complex, or extended reasoning. Explaining something in a content area that is more procedural could demand students to recall by applying concepts, knowledge, and skills; to think strategically; or think extensively about how to do something. Learning taxonomies such as Bloom's list multiple cognitive action verbs under their levels—to address, assess, and align to the specific mental processing skills that different content areas demand students perform.

Judging the complexity or quality of an academic standard, activity, or assessment based on the verb is not necessarily wrong. In fact, Webb (1999) identifies certain cognitive action verbs as *key words* that signify a certain level of cognitive demand or Depth of Knowledge. However, he also emphasizes the level of Depth of Knowledge should not be designated "without further clarification of the underlying intent of the [verb]" (Webb, 1999, p. 23). That intent is clarified by the words and phrases that follow the cognitive action verb and complete the learning intention or target statement. That's what Depth of Knowledge considers when determining the cognitive demand of academic standards, activities, and assessments.

Depth of Knowledge Is Demanding, Not Difficult

Depth of Knowledge is not based on how much students will learn or how well students will demonstrate their learning; that's item or task difficulty, not cognitive demand. Table 1.1 shows the difference between difficulty and demand.

Difficulty is subjective. What one student may find hard may seem easy to another. Difficulty is also subject to change. An activity, item, or task can become easier as students become more familiar with the subject. It can also be made easier if the teacher increases the amount of time or decreases the number of activities, items, or tasks

TABLE 1.1: Difficulty Versus Demand (DOK)

Item or Task Difficulty	Cognitive Demand (DOK)
• How easy or hard—or difficult—is the activity, item, or task?	• How simple, complex, or involved is the activity, item, or task?
• How much time and effort will it take students to complete the activity, item, or task?	• What is the complexity of the content knowledge students must learn?
• How many activities, items, or tasks must the students complete correctly within a specific timeframe?	• How deeply must students demonstrate their learning in a certain context?
• How confident do the students feel in their ability to complete the activity, item, or task correctly?	• What is the demand of the task students must complete?
• What is the percentage or proportion of students who responded correctly to specific or series of activities, items, or tasks?	• What is the demand of the specific mental processing students must perform?
	• What is the demand of the response students must provide?

students must complete. The demand of an academic standard, activity, or assessment remains constant even as students become more familiar with the content. For example, a student could view a complex activity, item, or task as hard initially. However, it could become easier as the student develops and deepens their knowledge and skills.

There's no 1:1 correspondence between difficulty and demand. For example, an activity or assessment might require a lower level of cognitive demand because it only requires students to recall information or how to use procedures to answer correctly. The level of difficulty, however, could depend on how many activities, items, or tasks students must complete, how much time they have, or how well they understand the text, topic, or technique. Conversely, students may be assigned a single activity, item, or task that's complex but easy because they have the time or feel they possess the mental processing needed to perform successfully.

When determining the Depth of Knowledge demanded by an academic standard, activity, or assessment, don't base it on how much students must learn. Consider what exactly students must learn, and how deeply students must demonstrate their learning. The more extensively students must understand and use their knowledge and skills in a certain context, the deeper the Depth of Knowledge demanded.

Webb's DOK Levels—Not Another Taxonomy

Depth of Knowledge features a model that categorizes the different contexts—or levels—students could understand and use in their learning. Table 1.2 (page 17) outlines the criteria of the four DOK levels. It includes the measures of the Depth of Knowledge (DOK) Model of Cognitive Complexity that Dr. Norman L. Webb developed with the Florida Department of Education (2008) to determine the cognitive demand of Florida's state standards and assessment. Florida's DOK model consisted of three levels instead of four, merging DOK 3 and DOK 4 into one level. They also coded the cognitive demand of their standards and assessments as low (DOK 1), moderate (DOK 2), or high (DOK 3 or 4). I added the measure "extensive" to describe the cognitive demand of a DOK 4 academic standard, activity, or assessment. I also created the DOK descriptors featured in the columns that specify the demand of the task students must complete, the mental processing students must perform, the response students must provide, and the goal and expectation for students. These descriptors provide the language we will use to consider and communicate the Depth of Knowledge demanded by an academic standard, activity, or assessment. The descriptors also clarify what exactly and confirm how deeply students must understand and use the knowledge in a DOK teaching and learning experience. (We'll delve deeper into these DOK descriptors in chapter 6, page 101.)

Webb's DOK levels do not function as a taxonomy. They do not build on each other or scaffold as stages or steps. Webb (2002) calls the levels *nominative*, describing four different and deeper ways students can understand and use their knowledge and skills as part of a teaching and learning experience. He also clarifies the DOK levels are categories, not classifications or measures (Webb, 2015a–c; Webb, 2019). They define and designate the demand of academic standards, curricular activities, and assessment items. They also describe the range, depth, and extent students could apply, connect, express, or transfer their learning.

Webb's DOK levels do not consider the difficulty of academic standards, activities, or assessments. In fact, students may find it more difficult to achieve a DOK 1 learning intention or target because it requires them to recall from memory a vast amount of information or how to use procedures to answer correctly. Conversely, an activity, item, or task that prompts students to think strategically (DOK 3) or extensively (DOK 4) may be easy for students once they acquire and develop the content knowledge they need to succeed. You also don't have to start at a reduced DOK level to get to a deeper one. Students should also be prompted and supported to demonstrate their learning at or beyond the DOK level demanded by a specific academic standard, curricular activity, or assessment item. However, one DOK level should not be considered better or more desirable than another. Each DOK level serves an important purpose and role in the development and demonstration of student learning.

TABLE 1.2: DOK Levels

What is the DOK level?	What is the cognitive demand?	What is the demand of the task students must complete?	What is the demand of the mental processing students must perform?	What is the demand of response students must provide?	What is the demand of the goal and expectation for students?
DOK 1 (recall)	Low	Just the facts Just do it	Recall information Recall how to	Answer correctly	Answer it
DOK 2 (skill or concept)	Moderate	Show and share or summarize Comprehend and communicate Specify and explain Give examples and non-examples	Apply knowledge, concepts, or skills Use information and basic reasoning	Establish and explain with examples	Use it to explain it
DOK 3 (strategic thinking)	High	Delve deeply Inquire and investigate Critical thinking Problem solving Creative thinking Defend, justify, or refute with evidence Connect, confirm, conclude, consider, or critique	Think strategically Use complex reasoning supported by evidence	Examine and explain with evidence	Use it to prove it
DOK 4 (extended thinking)	Extensive	Go deep within a subject area Go among texts and topics Go across the curriculum Go beyond the classroom	Use extended reasoning supported by expertise Think extensively	Explore and explain with examples and evidence (over an extended period)	Go for it

Webb's DOK levels are also not developmental pedagogically. Students at any age or grade level can demonstrate their learning at any DOK level. For example, preschoolers can be engaged and encouraged to think strategically at a DOK 3 or think extensively at a DOK 4. Graduate students can be required to only recall information or do something at a DOK 1. The same applies to student competency. Ability, age, or grade level should never be a factor or reason not to demand students to understand or use their learning at any DOK level.

The following sections (1) elaborate on how to use Webb's DOK levels, and (2) introduce the DOK blocks, the model I have created to transform the DOK levels into a multitiered, accessible system teachers can use to plan and provide teaching and learning experiences.

How to Use the DOK Levels

Depth of Knowledge and Webb's DOK levels were not intended to be an academic concept or framework for teaching and learning. Webb (1997) originally developed Depth of Knowledge as one of six criteria for analyzing the alignment of the content focus between expectations (standards) and assessments. According to Webb (1999), standards and assessments are aligned—or consistent—for Depth of Knowledge "if what is elicited from students on the assessment is as demanding cognitively as what students are expected to know and do as stated in the standards" (pp. 8–9). He initially developed the DOK levels as a coding system teachers and test makers could use to categorize and compare the degree of alignment—or DOK consistency—between grade-level standards and assessment activities, items, or tasks.

Figure 1.1 adapts Webb's scales of agreement for DOK consistency. I added the rating *Beyond* for activities, items, and tasks that demand students to demonstrate their learning beyond the DOK level of a standard's learning intention or its most cognitively demanding objective. According to Webb (1997), "Expectations and assessments will be fully aligned [for Depth of Knowledge] if both are cognitively complex or both are cognitively simple. How closely a comparison between expectations and assessments can be made will depend on the specificity of the expectations" (p. 16). Again, that's why Depth of Knowledge involves looking at the words and phrases beyond the initial cognitive action verb—to verify what exactly and how deeply students must understand and use their learning to demonstrate proficiency or perform successfully.

Like the DOK levels, the degrees of DOK consistency are not value judgements. All activities, items, and tasks that address or assess a standard—regardless of their DOK level—serve an important purpose in the education and evaluation of students. They

Insufficient	An activity, item, or task addresses and assesses the instructional focus of the academic standard but not at the level of cognitive complexity or demand of its learning intention.
Full	An activity, item, or task addresses and assesses the learning intention of the academic standard completely or addresses the most cognitively demanding objective within the standard's learning intention.
Acceptable	An activity, item, or task addresses and assesses at least 50 percent of the learning intention of the academic standard or demands students to demonstrate their learning at least one DOK level below the standard.
Beyond	An activity, item, or task demands students to demonstrate their learning beyond the level of Depth of Knowledge of the standard's learning intention and targets.

Source: Adapted from Webb, 1997.

Figure 1.1: DOK consistency criteria for alignment studies.

provide an accurate and authentic measure of the depth and extent of students' learning. That's why an activity, item, or task that's deemed unacceptable or insufficiently aligned to a standard should not be discredited nor disregarded. Students should also not be judged nor penalized for not being able to complete an activity, item, or task that assesses their learning beyond the standard's DOK level.

Educators can also use the DOK levels to measure the cognitive rigor of academic standards, curricular activities, and assessment items. Cognitive rigor is an academic concept developed by Karin Hess, who superimposed Webb's DOK levels with Bloom's revised taxonomy in matrix form to distinguish the difference between the two academic frameworks. The result was the Hess Cognitive Rigor Matrix (CRM), a resource and tool that "assist[s] teachers in applying what cognitive demand might look like in the classroom and guide[s] test developers in designing and aligning test items and performance tasks" (Hess, 2018, p. 43).

Figure 1.2 (page 20) is an example of the Hess CRM. The rows indicate the levels of thinking teachers can expect students to demonstrate as categorized by Bloom's revised taxonomy. The columns designate the depth and extent to which teachers can expect students to demonstrate their learning according to Webb's DOK levels. The placement of the learning intention or task in the Hess CRM codes its cognitive rigor. For example, all the learning intentions featured in figure 1.2 are placed in the second row of the matrix because *explaining* is a subcategory under the level *Understand* in

BLOOM'S REVISED TAXONOMY	WEBB'S DOK LEVELS			
	DOK 1 Recall and reproduce	**DOK 2** Concepts and skills or basic reasoning	**DOK 3** Strategic thinking or complex reasoning	**DOK 4** Extended thinking and reasoning
Remember				
Understand		Explain the difference between solids, liquids, and gases in terms of density, using the particle theory of matter. (BLOOM 2, DOK 2)	Explain why addition and subtraction strategies work, using place value and the properties of operations. (BLOOM 3, DOK 3)	Explain how the perspectives of people in the present shape interpretations of the past. (BLOOM 2, DOK 4)
Apply				
Analyze				
Evaluate				
Create				

Source: Adapted from Hess, 2005b.

Figure 1.2: Adapted Hess CRM with DOK descriptors.

Bloom's Revised Taxonomy (Anderson & Krathwohl, 2001). That's why they are all coded a BLOOM's 2. The DOK level demanded by each learning intention depends on the column it is placed in.

Notice some boxes in the Hess CRM are darkened. That's because certain cognitive actions do not demand students understand or use the content knowledge in certain contexts. For example, learning targets and tasks that expect students to remember will not demand students to demonstrate their learning beyond a DOK 1. Conversely, learning targets and tasks that expect students to evaluate will demand students to think strategically (DOK 3) or extensively (DOK 4). Keep in mind that it's the complexity of the content knowledge and context that govern into which column the learning target or task is placed in the Hess CRM.

To mark and measure the cognitive rigor of an academic standard, activity, or assessment, first identify the type of thinking the learning intention, objective, or target expects students to demonstrate and the level it's categorized in Bloom's. That decides the row it's placed in the matrix. Then verify what exactly and how deeply students must understand and use their learning according to the words and phrases following the learning intention, objective, or target's verb. That designates the DOK level and decides its placement in the columns of the matrix. Code the cognitive rigor based on the number of the Bloom row in the Hess CRM and DOK level.

Hess (2005a, 2006, 2018) also recommends using the DOK levels to establish assessment ceilings and ranges—especially with standardized assessments. The level of Depth of Knowledge demanded by an academic standard establishes the DOK ceiling of assessment. The ceiling is the deepest level to which test items assessing a specific standard could and should demand students demonstrate their learning. However, Hess (2018) warns against testing students only at the DOK ceiling of assessment or treating the DOK levels as testing targets. Doing so could make the assessment too difficult for students. It could also deny important information about the depth and extent of students' learning and the possible gaps they may have. She recommends administering test items that evaluate student learning over a range of DOK levels leading to the DOK ceiling of assessment. For example, if an academic standard is a DOK 3, the assessment should include test items that evaluate student learning at and up to that DOK level. This will make the assessment fair and balanced. It will also help with assessing strengths and addressing gaps in students' learning.

Though the DOK levels can be used to establish assessment ceilings and ranges, they should not be used as a scale for evaluating student performance or proficiency. Many grade and proficiency scales use letters or a four-point system to evaluate student performance. However, a DOK 4 is not equivalent to a score of 4 or a grade of an A, and a DOK 1 is not a 1 or a D. A student who achieves a learning intention or target at the level of Depth of Knowledge demanded should receive the highest score possible on a grade or proficiency scale. For example, if the learning intention or target is a DOK 1 and a student achieves it completely and successfully, then they should receive the highest score possible on the grading or proficiency scale. This is why I discourage using the DOK levels as a proficiency scale for standards-based grading. When it comes to teaching and learning for DOK and standards-based grading, levels of four do not translate into scales of four.

DOK Blocks

Figure 1.3 (page 23) is a visual I created that depicts the nominative nature and structure of the DOK levels as blocks. Each individual DOK block describes a definitive and distinct way students can understand and use their learning. They set the level of Depth of Knowledge demanded by a specific academic standard, activity, or assessment. They also specify the range of DOK levels teachers could teach and students should reach in a single teaching and learning experience. However, the DOK blocks are not steps and should not be treated or used as such.

The DOK blocks do not turn the DOK levels into a taxonomy. Instead, they transform the DOK levels into a multitiered system of supports (MTSS) for delivering instruction, responding to intervention, and extending student learning. Figure 1.4 (page 24) takes a closer look at an individual DOK block and how it informs the delivery and intensity of a DOK teaching and learning experience based on the demand of the standard and the strengths of the students. The top of the block is the ceiling of assessment. That's established by the level of Depth of Knowledge demanded by a standard's learning intention. I call this the *DOK bar* because this is the goal and expectation of a DOK teaching and learning experience—for all students to rise to, reach, and go beyond the level of Depth of Knowledge (or the DOK bar) demanded by a learning intention, objective, or target.

The DOK bar is represented as a dashed line because it's always moving throughout a DOK teaching and learning experience, changing its position based on the demand of the standard and the strengths of the student. The level of Depth of Knowledge demanded by a learning intention sets the DOK bar's initial placement.

The right side of the DOK block is the pathway to proficiency. It outlines how teachers deliver their instruction—or move the DOK bar—throughout a DOK teaching and learning experience. The pathway to proficiency can go in either direction, which is why the sides of the DOK block are double-sided arrows. The left side of the DOK block maps the progression of performance for students, which always leads to and beyond the level of Depth of Knowledge demanded by the standard's learning intention or target. The arrows on both sides of the DOK block and the direction they point show how to develop and deliver a DOK teaching and learning experience that is standards-based and student-centered. It also provides a balance between proficiency-based and competency-based learning.

The inverted pyramid within the DOK block shows how the delivery and intensity of a DOK teaching and learning experience are both standards-based and student-centered. The inverted pyramid is based on the RTI at Work™ model and process developed by Austin Buffum, Mike Mattos, and Janet Malone (2018). It shows how the delivery and intensity of the instruction address and assess both the demand of a standard's learning intention and the specific strengths and needs of students individually and collectively as a class or grade level. It also shows how the teacher adjusts and

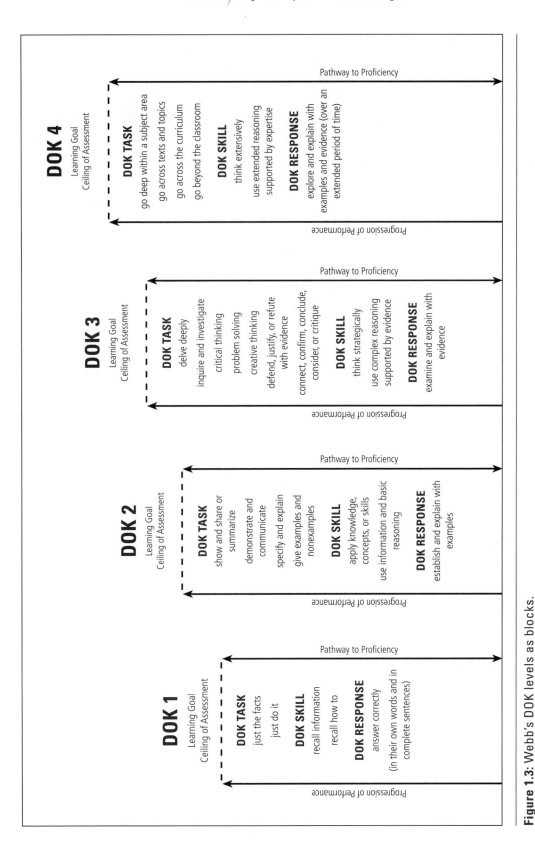

Figure 1.3: Webb's DOK levels as blocks.

Visit go.SolutionTree.com/instruction for a free reproducible version of this figure.

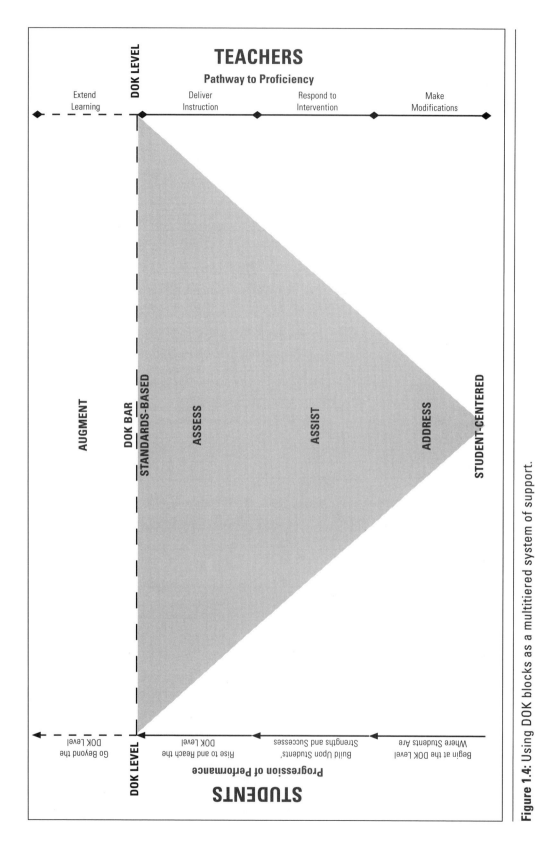

Figure 1.4: Using DOK blocks as a multitiered system of support.

Visit go.SolutionTree.com/instruction for a free reproducible version of this figure.

modifies—or tiers—their instruction to assist and augment students' learning as they progress toward achieving and surpassing the proficiency goals and expectations set by the standards and the personal goals students set for themselves.

I will feature and reference the DOK blocks throughout the book, using them as examples and evidence that explain the specific ideas and strategies established, examined, and explored in the subsequent chapters.

Summary

Knowing the type and level of thinking an academic standard, activity, or assessment expects students to demonstrate is half the battle. We need to confirm the depth of content understanding students must develop to demonstrate grade-level proficiency. We also need to clarify the extent to which students must use the subject-specific knowledge and skills to perform successfully. We find this clarification in the words and phrases that follow the initial cognitive action verb of a learning intention or target. Those words and phrases determine the Depth of Knowledge an academic standard, activity, or assessment demands.

Webb's DOK levels describe the different and deeper contexts in which students could demonstrate their learning. These levels do not function as a taxonomy. They serve as a system for coding and comparing the degree of alignment between expectations and assessments. They mark and measure the cognitive rigor of curricular activities and test items along with Bloom's revised taxonomy. They establish the ceiling and the range for which test items can assess and evaluate student learning. They can also be used as a method and model to inform ideas about delivering instruction, responding to intervention, and extending student learning to and beyond the DOK level demanded by a standard's learning intention or target.

Understanding Depth of Knowledge

Either on your own or as part of a teacher team, reflect on and respond to the following questions.

- How could you use the DOK levels to confirm the cognitive demand of academic standards, activities, and assessments?

- How could you use the DOK levels as a coding system to determine the degree of alignment between academic standards, activities, and assessments?

- How could you use the DOK levels along with Bloom's revised taxonomy to measure the cognitive rigor of learning targets and tasks?

- How could you use the DOK levels to establish assessment ceilings and ranges for test items that address a specific academic standard?

- How could you use the DOK levels along with the learning taxonomy you currently use to develop and deliver teaching and learning experiences that will demand students demonstrate their learning in different contexts?

CHAPTER TWO

What Are DOK Teaching and Learning Experiences?

In chapter 1 (page 9), we learned what Depth of Knowledge is and how the DOK levels describe four different contexts in which students can understand and use their learning. We also learned that Webb's DOK levels (along with Bloom's revised taxonomy) mark and measure the cognitive rigor of academic standards, activities, and assessment items. But what distinguishes the rigor of DOK teaching and learning experiences? How can you use the DOK levels to plan and provide teaching and learning experiences that are academically rigorous, socially and emotionally supportive, and student responsive?

To answer these questions, this chapter provides information on how to develop and deliver DOK teaching and learning experiences that focus on the following four points: (1) knowledge acquisition, (2) knowledge application, (3) knowledge analysis, and (4) knowledge augmentation. This chapter also discusses teacher and student roles and responsibilities and presents appropriate examples of teaching activities and experiences. The chapter concludes with reflection questions to allow you to assess your understanding of Depth of Knowledge to this point.

How to Develop DOK Teaching and Learning Experiences

Teaching and learning for Depth of Knowledge demand students do the following.

- Acquire the foundational knowledge and skills required to answer questions, solve problems, complete tasks, or understand texts and topics correctly.

- Apply conceptual and procedural understanding accurately to answer questions, address problems, accomplish tasks, or analyze a text or topic.

- Analyze how and why acquired knowledge could be used as evidence to justify answers, actions, analyses, alternatives, or arguments—their own or those presented by others.

- Augment knowledge by exploring and explaining how they could transfer, use, and connect their learning deep within a subject, among texts or topics, across the curriculum, beyond the classroom, and in their own unique ways.

Figure 2.1 uses the DOK blocks introduced in chapter 1 to summarize the overarching goal and expectation of teaching and learning at each DOK level. Notice how each DOK block in the figure establishes and explains the overarching goal and expectation for a teaching and learning experience at each DOK level. The blocks also show how each DOK level plays an explicit and essential role in how teachers deliver their instruction and how students develop, demonstrate, and deepen their learning. One DOK level should not be considered "better" or "more desirable" than another. Also, the DOK level of a teaching and learning experience depends on the depth and extent students must understand and use their learning, not the specific strategy or pedagogical approach used to instruct, assess, or engage students. For example, constructivist instructional strategies such as inquiry-based and project-based learning are best practices teachers could use to engage students in deeper DOK teaching and learning experiences. However, it's the depth and extent to which the teaching and learning experience demands students to understand and use their learning that determine the DOK level, not the method or practice used.

DOK 1: Knowledge Acquisition

The goal and expectation of a DOK 1 teaching and learning experience are for students to acquire the foundational knowledge and functional understanding they need to succeed in a specific subject. Table 2.1 (page 30) details the roles and responsibilities of the teacher and students in a DOK 1 teaching and learning experience.

DOK 1 activities and assessments are routine and simple. Students must "demonstrate a rote response, use a well-known formula, follow a set procedure (like a recipe), or perform a clearly defined series of steps" (Webb, 2002, p. 5). No further explanation,

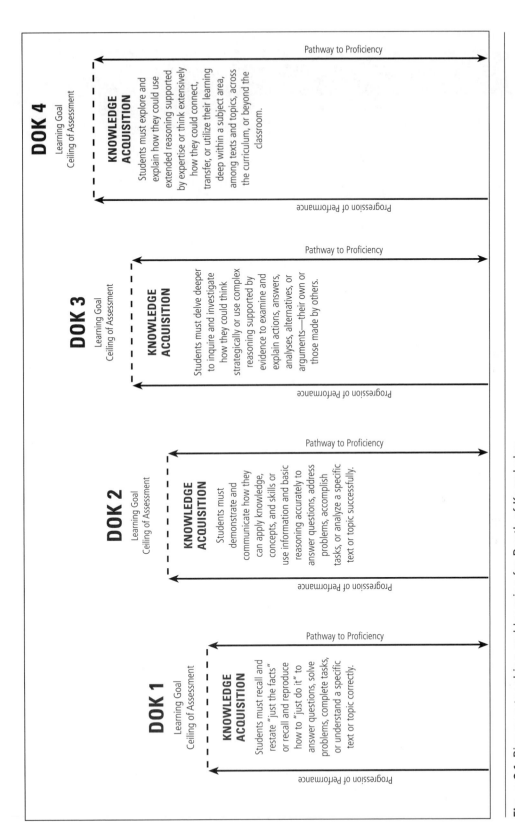

Figure 2.1: Rigorous teaching and learning for Depth of Knowledge.

Visit go.SolutionTree.com/instruction for a free reproducible version of this figure.

TABLE 2.1: DOK 1 Teacher and Student Roles and Responsibilities

Teacher Roles and Responsibilities	Student Roles and Responsibilities
• Directs and leads the teaching and learning experience • Shows and tells the specific information and procedures students must learn • Provides details, facts, or specifics • Presents directions, instructions, or steps • Asks questions to assess knowledge and check for understanding • Assesses and evaluates for correctness • Speaks for most of the experience	• Listens and observes attentively during the teaching and learning experience • Memorizes the specific information or procedures teachers have taught • Recalls details, facts, or specifics correctly • Follows directions, instructions, or steps correctly • Asks questions to develop background knowledge and basic understanding • Answers correctly or incorrectly • Speaks when called on or has a question

justification, or extension are demanded. Students are required to recall just the facts or how to do something as correctly and explicitly as it's taught by the teacher or a text. However, this doesn't mean DOK 1 curricular activities and test items are easy or basic. In fact, these lessons and assessments can be the most difficult for students, especially as they begin to learn about a subject. The following list includes examples of DOK 1 activities, items, and tasks that require students to recall information or procedures (Hess, 2015a–c; Webb, 2014a–c, 2019).

- Recall data, definitions, details, elements, facts, or information.

- Support ideas with reference to verbatim (or only slightly paraphrased) details from the text.

- Use a dictionary to find the meanings of words.

- Recognize figurative language in a reading passage.

- Identify, label, or locate data, information, or parts in a print or visual text.

- Recognize or identify specific information contained in maps, charts, tables, graphs, drawings, or other graphics.

- Define the meaning of words, phrases, or terms using a dictionary, glossary, or thesaurus.

- Describe or explain who, what, where, when, how, or why according to a source or text.

- Memorize facts, information, operations, or procedures.

- Read and recite lines fluently and accurately from a text or from memory.

- Solve a routine and simple problem with a single or specific outcome, result, or solution.

- Complete a simple task successfully.

- Perform a one-step computation or operation.

- Apply a direct or specific algorithm, formula, or routine procedure.

- Execute or follow a well-defined multistep procedure.

- Respond yes or no.

- Declare a statement as true or false.

- Make a list.

- Identify patterns, trends, causes, or effects.

- Complete a word search or crossword puzzle.

- Brainstorm ideas related to the specific text or topic being studied.

According to Hess's Cognitive Rigor Matrix (see figure 1.2, page 20), DOK 1 teaching and learning experiences could expect students to demonstrate higher levels of thinking. For example, activities and assessments could require students to analyze by identifying patterns or trends or locating and retrieving information from a specific print or visual text (for example, maps, charts, or tables). They could require students to answer a question, solve a problem, or complete a task correctly (Hess, 2013c; Hess et al., 2010a, 2010b). Students might create by brainstorming ideas, concepts, or perspectives related to a specific text or topic (Hess et al., 2010a, 2010b). However, even though students are expected to think deeply, DOK 1 activities or assessment items will only demand students to recall the facts or how to do something without offering deeper explanations, interpretations, or further exploration. They do not have to be "figured out" or "solved" (Petit & Hess, 2006; Webb, 2002, 2015a).

DOK 1 teaching and learning experiences also focus on students acquiring basic literacy and language skills. Students learn the print concepts and the conventions of a target language (for example, phonemic sounds, spelling of words, word meaning, part of speech, sentence structure, and word placement). They are also introduced to the terminology of a specific subject—the verbal and nonverbal labels and symbols "used by experts to express what they know [and] communicate with others in their discipline" (Anderson & Krathwohl, 2001, p. 45). Activities and assessments demand students to demonstrate "a shallow understanding of the text presented and often consist of verbatim recall from text, slight paraphrasing of specific details from the text, or simple understanding of a single word or phrase" (Webb, 2015b, p. 1). Again, no deeper explanation, evaluation, or extension is demanded. Students must only recall and restate information or reproduce procedures correctly and explicitly as they are presented or printed in a specific text.

A DOK 1 teaching and learning experience can be difficult for students, especially when they are first learning about the text, topic, or technique. The level of difficulty may change as students become more familiar with the subject. However, the cognitive demand of a DOK 1 teaching and learning experience will remain low because it only requires students to recall *just the facts* or to demonstrate how to *just do it* correctly. This is also what you tell students when they ask what's expected of them in a DOK 1 teaching and learning experience—recall just the facts or demonstrate how to just do it correctly.

DOK 2: Knowledge Application

The goal and expectation of a DOK 2 teaching and learning experience is for students to comprehend and communicate how and why they can apply the content knowledge to answer questions, address problems, accomplish tasks, or analyze the ideas and information presented in texts or pertaining to topics. Table 2.2 describes the roles and responsibilities of the teacher and student in a DOK 2 teaching and learning experience.

DOK 2 activities and assessments demand students to understand and use the content knowledge correctly. However, according to Webb (2002), "The content knowledge and processes involved are more complex than in [DOK 1]" (p. 5). Students learn how to organize and apply information and procedures as categories and criteria, methods and models, structures and skills, or theories and techniques. Activities and assessments also challenge students to use their deeper understanding to make choices, comparisons, and connections. The following list features examples of DOK 2 activities, items, and tasks that will challenge students to show and share their deeper understanding of concepts, ideas, and processes (Hess, 2013a–g; Webb, 2015a–c, 2019).

- Describe, explain, or interpret how or why.

- Explain the series of steps completed, taken, or used to find a solution.

- Summarize ideas or information with supporting examples.

- Draw meaning from text by using organizational structure, examples, and context.

- Follow cause-and-effect sequences and multiple ideas through a text.

- Distinguish among hypotheses and givens as well as fact from opinion.

- Explain differences among genres (poetry, expository materials, fiction, and so on).

TABLE 2.2: DOK 2 Teacher and Student Roles and Responsibilities

Teacher Roles and Responsibilities	Student Roles and Responsibilities
• Assigns and guides the teaching and learning experience	• Participates actively in the teaching and learning experience
• Steps back to observe and oversee student performance	• Speaks up to show and share or summarize
• Prompts students to demonstrate and communicate how they can use the content knowledge accurately to answer questions, address problems, accomplish tasks, or analyze texts and topics	• Demonstrates and communicates how they use the content knowledge accurately to answer questions, address problems, accomplish tasks, or analyze the ideas and information presented in a specific text or pertaining to a particular topic
• Asks questions to check for conceptual or procedural understanding or to understand students' actions, answers, or analyses	• Asks questions to develop conceptual or procedural understanding or to clarify actions, answers, or analyses
• Assesses and evaluates students' responses, results, or reasoning based on correctness and clarity	• Establishes and explains responses, results, or reasoning with supporting examples correctly and clearly

- Use context cues to identify the meaning of unfamiliar words, phrases, and expressions that could otherwise have multiple meanings.

- Predict a logical outcome based on information in a reading selection.

- Identify and summarize the major events in a narrative.

- Categorize or classify data and information based on specific criteria.

- Compare or contrast people, places, events, and concepts based on characteristics.

- Convert information from one form to another.

- Formulate an equation or inequality, derive a solution, and report the solution.

- Perform a routine experiment with two or more steps that produces a specific result.

- Select a method or procedure according to what the task requires and perform it.

- Conduct an experiment with a specific outcome, result, or solution.

- Construct or use a model or visual to explain a concept, idea, phenomenon, or process.

- Solve routine problems involving multiple decision points or methods.

- Choose from options given.

- Make basic inferences or logical predictions based on data and information provided.

- Obtain and interpret information using context, text features, or visuals.

- Generate conjectures or hypotheses based on experience or observations.

- Explain or extend a pattern or trend.

- Make a diorama that illustrates or explains an actual or fictional event.

- Conduct an interview that prompts someone to explain or express ideas or perspectives.

- Create a questionnaire or survey that gathers quantitative or qualitative data.

- Write a journal, diary, or blog to express and explain beliefs, feelings, ideas, or opinions.

A DOK 1 item or task could be used in a DOK 2 teaching and learning experience. However, the activity or assessment must challenge students "to go beyond a description or explanation of recalled information to describe or explain a result or 'how' or 'why'" (Webb, 2002, p. 8). For example, in mathematics, instead of simply solving problems correctly, students must show and share or summarize how they used a concept, operation, or procedure to attain their answer. In literature and the arts, instead of simply identifying literary or artistic devices, students must use information and basic reasoning to explain the main or explicit ideas in a text or work and how the author, artist, or musician used the elements of craft and structure to express those ideas. In history or social studies, instead of simply creating a timeline, students must specify and explain the connections between the events. In world language, instead of simply identifying the correct form or tense, students must apply knowledge, concepts, and skills to explain how the form or tense is used in a communication or conversation. In physical education, instead of simply throwing a particular pitch in baseball, students must establish and explain with examples how the pitch is or can be thrown. Successful student performance depends on how correctly and clearly students apply and articulate their learning in the assigned context.

DOK 2 teaching and learning experiences apply a content-area literacy approach to instruction and assessment. Ramona Chauvin and Kathleen Theodore (2015) describe content-area literacy as "the ability to use reading and writing to learn the subject matter in a discipline" (p. 2). The instructional focus and purpose shift from learning how to read, write, and discuss to reading, writing, and discussing to learn. This should happen in all subjects at all grade levels, not just literature or language arts classes at the secondary level. With a content-area literacy approach, students are challenged to read and respond to informational texts in different disciplines to deepen their conceptual and procedural understanding of the content knowledge. They must also use the information from these texts and basic reasoning to communicate their understanding by paraphrasing, specifying, or summarizing. They also interpret or construct meaning from texts and about topics based on the information provided or how it is presented (Webb, 2015b). Table 2.3 (page 36) features examples of reading tasks and writing-to-learn activities for DOK 2 teaching and learning experiences for all subjects. Victoria Gillis (2014) recommends adapting rather than adopting these activities and tasks to address the content and communication focus of the specific subject. For example, students may use transition words commonly used in mathematics or science to detail or document a phenomenon or process.

The simplest way to deepen a teaching and learning experience to a DOK 2 is to challenge students to demonstrate and communicate their learning (or with the younger students, "show and share"). However, students must express and share their understanding in their own words. This is what makes the DOK 2 teaching and learning experience more challenging and cognitively demanding.

DOK 3: Knowledge Analysis

The goal and expectation of DOK 3 teaching and learning experiences are to deepen students' awareness of how and why they could use the content knowledge in different contexts. Table 2.4 (page 37) explains the roles and responsibilities of the teacher and student in DOK 3 teaching and learning experiences.

DOK 3 activities and assessments are highly complex and abstract. Students use strategic thinking and complex reasoning to examine and explain answers, actions, analyses, alternatives, or arguments—their own or those presented by others. What distinguishes DOK 3 activities and assessments is they demand students understand and use the content knowledge as evidence to strengthen and support calculations, claims, conclusions, or conjectures. According to Webb (2015c), students "go beyond knowing how and why to justifying the how and why through application and evidence" (p. 2). The following list features examples of DOK 3 activities, items, and tasks that engage students to use strategic thinking and complex reasoning (Hess, 2013a–g; Webb, 2015a–c, 2019).

- Explain, generalize, or connect ideas using supporting evidence.
- Justify actions, answers, analyses, alternatives, and arguments with supporting evidence.

TABLE 2.3: Content-Area Literary Skills

Reading Tasks	Writing-to-Learn Activities
• Cite or paraphrase specific details, facts, and information from literary and informational texts to make and support explanations, inferences, or predictions. • Determine the main, central, or explicit ideas expressed in a literary or informational text. • Summarize the key details and ideas of a literary or informational text (for example, main ideas, character traits, plots, or themes). • Identify, explain, and trace the steps for a process detailed in a literary or informational text. • Use context clues to determine the meaning of general academic or literary words and subject-specific terminology. • Describe how an informational text presents details, facts, and information. • Identify aspects of the text that reveal the author's purpose or point of view. • Distinguish between relevant and irrelevant information, facts and opinions, and primary and secondary sources. • Explain differences among genres and types of texts. • Understand and use the conventions, format, style, or terminology of a specific subject to read and respond to a literary or informational text (for example, lab reports, historical documents, athletic playbooks, musical lyrics, or stage plays or screenplays).	• Write generic or focused summaries to understand texts, topics, or techniques more clearly. • Write informative or explanatory texts that explain concepts, events, ideas, or processes. • Write narratives that summarize the sequence of events of experiences or phenomena from start to finish. • Write responses that express personal beliefs, feelings, opinions, perspectives, or thoughts about a text or topic. • Use technical writing (step 1, step 2, step 3 . . .) to detail or document the stages or steps of a phenomenon or process. • Use transitional words (first . . ., next . . ., then . . ., finally . . .) to detail or document the stages or steps of a phenomenon or process. • Keep a learning log or reader-response journal that records reactions, reflections, or responses to a text or topic. • Write letters, notes, or text messages to explain concepts, events, ideas, or processes. • Understand and use the conventions, format, style, or terminology of a specific subject to write and produce a literary or informational text (for example, MLA or APA format, lab reports, mathematical proofs, musical lyrics, or stage plays or screenplays).

- Cite textual evidence to strengthen and support claims, conclusions, or conjectures.

- Critique actions, conclusions, or decisions based on credibility of evidence or sources.

TABLE 2.4: DOK 3 Teacher and Student Roles and Responsibilities

Teacher Roles and Responsibilities	Student Roles and Responsibilities
• Moderates and monitors the learning experience	• Engages deeply in the learning experience
• Presents a complex goal or task with specific criteria or stipulations students must achieve	• Uses deep knowledge and skills to achieve the criteria or stipulations of a goal or task
• Provides students with different contexts in which they could demonstrate their learning	• Examines and explains with evidence how they could demonstrate their learning in different contexts
• Engages students to think strategically or use complex reasoning supported by evidence to justify answers, actions, analyses, alternatives, or arguments—their own or those presented by others	• Thinks strategically or uses complex reasoning supported by evidence to justify answers, actions, analyses, alternatives, or arguments—their own or those presented by others
• Asks questions to stimulate deeper thinking, probe reasoning, or pique curiosity, imagination, interest, and wonder	• Asks questions to delve deeper or consider alternatives, causes, connections, consequences, options, outcomes, perspectives, or possibilities
• Assesses and evaluates student learning based on correctness, clarity, and credibility of evidence and reasoning	• Uses evidence and reasoning correctly, clearly, and credibly to strengthen and support responses and results

- Explain or recognize how the author's purpose affects the interpretation of a reading selection.

- Conduct analyses of the text to make inferences about an author's purpose and use of textual features.

- Summarize information from multiple sources to address a specific topic.

- Analyze and describe the characteristics of various types of literature.

- Evaluate ideas, performance, or works based on craftsmanship, credibility, or criteria.

- Apply and analyze concepts and processes to solve nonroutine or ill-structured problems.

- Use decision making, troubleshooting, or a diagnosis-solution method to address a problem.

- Analyze similarities and differences among issues and problems.

- Propose and evaluate solutions to problems.

- Recognize and explain misconceptions.

- Make connections across time and place to explain a concept or big idea.

- Monitor performance and adjust methods, strategies, or techniques if necessary.

- Consider alternatives, consequences, options, or possibilities.

- Verify and validate the reasonableness of results.

- Develop and use a model or visual to explain a concept, idea, phenomenon, or process.

- Conduct an investigation for a specific purpose or one that addresses a research question.

- Draw conclusions based on recorded or reported data, information, observations, or results.

- Address a complex problem or accomplish a complex task within a specific time limit.

- Analyze and evaluate the impact or effectiveness of a policy or procedure.

- Compile and synthesize information from a single source or text.

- Write and prepare an informational text, report, or presentation on a specific subject.

- Initiate and participate in a debate, dialogue, or discussion.

- Respond to document-based questions that address and examine the universal ideas and themes presented in a single text of literary fiction or pertaining to a topic.

- Engage in a problem-based or project-based learning experience with a definitive outcome or specific time limit.

DOK 3 teaching and learning experiences also engage students to develop and demonstrate the complex mental processing skills—or competencies—that will benefit them in school and society. Figure 2.2 (page 40) lists what Bernie Trilling and Charles Fadel (2009) identify as the four Cs of 21st century learning—the set of critical learning and innovation skills and subskills essential for success and survival in learning, life, and the labor force. The learning intentions associated with these competencies are applicable and adaptable for DOK 3 teaching and learning experiences of all subjects at all grade levels. The learning intentions associated with these competencies are applicable and adaptable for DOK 3 teaching and learning experiences of all subjects at all grade levels. They engage students to develop and demonstrate deeper academic and authentic knowledge and skills they need to succeed academically, professionally, and personally. When planning activities and assessments, include these core competencies as learning goals and expectations to make the DOK 3 teaching and learning experience both rigorous and relevant.

DOK 3 teaching and learning experiences employ a disciplinary literacy approach with instruction and assessment. According to Timothy and Cynthia Shanahan (2012), disciplinary literacy "emphasizes the specialized knowledge and abilities possessed by those who create, communicate, and use knowledge within each of the disciplines" (p. 7). These professional practices and specialized skills are addressed in a content area's anchor standards (for example, the Standards for Mathematical Practice, the Mathematics College and Career Readiness Standards, the Scientific and Engineering Practices and Crosscutting Concepts of the Next Generation Science Standards, the anchor standards of the Literacy and Language CCRS, the National Core Arts Standards, the AERO World Language Standards, and the SHAPE America Standards). DOK 3 activities and assessments engage students to address and respond to learning experiences as if they are participants or professionals in a particular area or field—a mathematician or scientist, literary, art, music, or theater critic, a historian, a language or linguistic specialist, or an athlete or coach.

DOK 1 and DOK 2 items and tasks could be assigned in a DOK 3 teaching and learning experience. However, the activity or assessment must engage students to "go beyond explaining or describing 'how and why' to justifying the 'how and why' through application and evidence" (Webb, 2002, p. 8). The simplest way to deliver a DOK 3 teaching and learning experience is to present students with an opinion, option, or outcome and engage them in confirming, concluding, considering, or critiquing its accuracy, validity, or viability. For example, in mathematics or science, instead of requiring students to solve problems, present students with a solution and engage them to justify whether it's correct or incorrect. In literature and the arts, instead of asking students what the central idea or theme is, share with students what the textbook or a credible source says is the idea or theme and challenge them to examine and explain with evidence from the text how those ideas or themes are strengthened and supported. Then ask them to use complex reasoning supported by evidence to explain what they believe the central idea or theme is and why. In physical education, present students with a scenario on the field or court, engage them to think strategically about which would be the best play to execute, and then have them examine and evaluate the effectiveness of the play. Successful student performance depends on whether the evidence and reasoning are clear, credible, and convincing.

FOUR Cs SKILL	DOK 3 LEARNING INTENTIONS
Critical Thinking and Problem Solving **(Expert thinking)**	• Solve routine and nonroutine problems in different contexts. • Use various types of reasoning based on the situation. • Analyze how parts of a whole interact with each other. • Analyze and evaluate arguments, beliefs, claims, perspectives, or points of view based on the credibility of the evidence. • Interpret information and draw conclusions based on the best analysis.
Creativity and Innovation **(Applied imagination and invention)**	• Come up with innovative or inventive ideas. • Analyze, evaluate, and refine ideas for improvement or potential. • Be open and responsive to new and diverse perspectives. • Understand the real-world limits to accepting or adopting new ideas. • Understand and view obstacles, rejection, or setbacks as an opportunity to learn. • Recognize and realize that creativity and innovation involve a long-term, cyclical process of successes and mistakes. • Act on creative ideas to make change or contributions.
Communication **(Complex engagement and interaction)**	• Articulate thoughts and ideas effectively using oral, written, and nonverbal communication in a variety of forms and contexts. • Communicate new ideas or information to others clearly and effectively. • Listen deeply to decipher meaning. • Use communication in different contexts and for a range of purposes. • Utilize multiple forms and types of communication and evaluate their effectiveness and impact.
Collaboration **(Complex engagement and interaction)**	• Work effectively and respectfully with others. • Exercise flexibility and willingness to be helpful, make changes, or make compromises to accomplish a common goal. • Assume shared responsibility for collaborative work, successes, and setbacks. • Value group and individual contributions made by each member.

Sources: Partnership for 21st Century Learning, 2019; Trilling & Fadel, 2009.

Figure 2.2: The four Cs of 21st century learning.

DOK 4: Knowledge Augmentation

The goal and expectation of a DOK 4 teaching and learning experience are to extend students' learning beyond the content, the curriculum, and the classroom. Table 2.5 describes the roles and responsibilities of the teacher and student in a DOK 4 teaching and learning experience.

TABLE 2.5: DOK 4 Teacher and Student Roles and Responsibilities

Teacher Roles and Responsibilities	Student Roles and Responsibilities
• Initiates, evaluates, and critiques the learning experience	• Proposes, plans, and presents the learning experience
• Prompts students to think extensively how they could use the knowledge in diverse contexts and unique situations	• Thinks extensively about how they could use the knowledge to address, explain, or respond to a real-world scenario or situation
• Provides opportunities for students to determine and discover how they could apply, connect, or transfer the knowledge within a subject area, across texts and topics, across the curriculum, beyond the classroom, or in their own unique way	• Explores and explains with examples and evidence how they could apply, connect, or transfer the knowledge within a subject area, across texts and topics, across the curriculum, beyond the classroom, or in their own unique way
• Encourages students to develop their learning, life experiences, and innate gifts into personal expertise	• Develops their learning, life experiences, and innate gifts into personal expertise to draw upon and use
• Assigns authentic, intricate, and time-consuming tasks requiring in-depth research and investigation, planning, or the design of an authentic product	• Completes authentic, intricate, and time-consuming tasks that involve in-depth research and investigation, planning, or the design of an authentic product

The complexity of DOK 3 and DOK 4 activities and assessments is similar. However, according to Hess (2013b), a DOK 3 activity or assessment demands students demonstrate "in-depth understanding of one text, one data set, one investigation, or one key source, whereas DOK 4 tasks expand the breadth of the task using multiple texts or sources, or multiple concepts/disciplines to reach a solution or create a final product" (p. 14). For example, in literature and the arts, instead of conducting a literary or style analysis for a single text or work, encourage students to conduct author, artist, or genre studies that demand they analyze the key details and ideas or craft and structure of multiple texts written by the same or different authors or produced by the same or different artist or musicians. In history or social studies, encourage students to explore and explain with examples and evidence the impact of ideas, incidents, individuals, or issues along a time continuum. The following list contains DOK 4 activities, items, and tasks that will encourage students to extend their learning (Hess, 2013a–g; Webb, 2015a–c, 2019).

- Explain how concepts or ideas connect or relate to other concepts or content within or across disciplines and subjects.

- Develop generalizations, perspectives, or theories based on outcomes or results attained or methods and strategies used and apply them in different contexts or new situations.

- Conduct in-depth investigations to establish connections between academic content or how the content can be used in real-world contexts.

- Analyze and synthesize information from multiple sources.

- Examine and explain alternative perspectives across a variety of sources.

- Describe and illustrate how common themes are found across texts from different cultures.

- Select or devise an approach from the alternatives, options, or possibilities provided to solve a nonroutine or novel problem.

- Analyze the common ideas, motifs, styles, and themes of multiple texts and works within or across genres or by the same or different author or artist.

- Initiate and participate in a project with no time constraints that involves in-depth research, experimentation, investigation, and design.

- Gather, analyze, evaluate, and synthesize ideas and information from multiple sources or texts and confirm their authenticity, credibility, or validity.

- Apply knowledge and skills in a new or novel way, explaining and justifying actions, decisions, and reasoning.

- Design and use an original model that addresses, explains, or responds to an abstract real-world scenario or situation.

- Create an original work of art, literature, or music that incorporates the key ideas, motifs, styles, or themes of a specific genre or pays homage to an author, artist, or musician.

- Respond to document-based questions that address and explore global or universal concepts, ideas, or themes.

DOK 4 teaching and learning experiences could take an extensive amount of time and effort to complete. However, these are a characteristic of DOK 4 activities and assessments, not a criterion. According to Webb (1999), "The extended time period is not a distinguishing factor if the required work is only repetitive and does not require applying significant conceptual understanding and [deeper mental processing]" (pp. 22–23). Such experiences could be designated a DOK 2 or DOK 3 depending on the depth and extent to which they demand students understand and use the content knowledge. That's why it's essential to consider what exactly and confirm how deeply the activity or assessment demands students to understand and use their learning before concluding its DOK level.

Figure 2.3 (page 44) features examples of specific curricular activities and instructional practices that could engage students in an extensive and involved DOK 4 teaching and learning experience. These experiences generally encourage students to "[employ and sustain] strategic thinking processes over a longer period of time to solve the problem or produce an authentic product" (Hess, 2013a, p. 18). However, keep in mind it's the depth and extent to which the teaching and learning experience demands students to understand and use their learning that designate it a DOK 4, not the specific pedagogical approach or instructional method used to plan or provide the experience.

The problems addressed in a DOK 4 teaching and learning experience could be tame or wicked. According to Horst Rittel and Melvin Webber (1973), *tame problems* are solved by applying an algorithm, formula, or process that has worked or been proven effective in a similar scenario or situation. *Wicked problems* cannot be addressed using clear-cut or conventional problem-solving processes. In fact, they are near impossible to address completely or solve successfully because there are so many interconnected causes, circumstances, components, and consequences. Examples of wicked problems include socioeconomic, political, cultural, or environmental issues involving education, poverty, financial stability and status, health care and wellness, crime, climate change, equity, social justice, and terrorism. Table 2.6 (page 45) distinguishes the characteristics of tame and wicked problems.

DOK 4 teaching and learning experiences also encourage students to think extensively how they could complete what Michael Dobson (2013) calls *impossible projects*. Impossible projects are like wicked problems "because of the many components, factors, individuals, and resources affected and involved" (Francis, 2016a, p. 162). Impossible projects can also be restrictive due to a lack of resources, time, or understanding. Space travel, splitting the atom, harnessing natural power (for example, electricity, wind, water, nuclear, or solar), curing diseases, constructing super architectural

STEM, STEAM, STREAM	Students incorporate and utilize the disciplinary literacies of science, technology, engineering, mathematics, reading and writing, and the arts to address, explain, and respond to real-world scenarios and situations.
Author or Genre Study	Students compare and critique the common elements of multiple texts of literary fiction or nonfiction addressing the same topic, written by the same or different authors, written within the same or different genres, or produced in different ways for different formats (for example, the film adaptation of a short story).
Case Study	Students conduct an in-depth analysis or intensive investigation of an incident, individual, or issue to draw conclusions and critique methods or outcomes using data and information from multiple sources.
Expeditionary Learning	Students take their learning beyond the classroom physically or virtually by conducting expeditions, fieldwork, or case studies.
Service Learning	Students address a civic, human, or social concern, issue, need, or situation within their own community to cause and create positive or productive change.
Personalized Learning	Students apply and associate academic content, concepts, and procedures with individual interests or to address, explain, and respond to issues and situations relevant to their lives.
Capstone Project	Students undertake a long-term investigative project that culminates with a final plan product, presentation, or performance given to a panel of teachers, experts, or community members who collectively evaluate its quality.
Exhibits, Productions, and Showcases	Students use their deep knowledge, innate gifts, trained talents, and creative thinking to plan and produce a performance or production that will be presented to an audience for evaluation or entertainment.

Figure 2.3: DOK 4 authentic learning experiences.

structures, and creating artificial intelligence were all impossible projects at one time. However, these all eventually became possible due to one person or group's patience and persistence. That's what distinguishes impossible projects from wicked problems. Wicked problems cannot be solved completely or successfully, but impossible problems could be completed successfully at some point. DOK 4 teaching and learning experiences inspire students to think extensively about how they could be innovative and inventive with the content knowledge and use the 4 Cs of 21st century learning to make what's considered impossible or fantastical practical or real.

So why bother encouraging students to explore wicked problems or impossible projects in a DOK 4 teaching and learning experience if these learning experiences are so extensive, exhausting, and even exasperating? Because according to Jon Kolko (2012),

TABLE 2.6: Tame vs. Wicked Problems

Tame Problems	Wicked Problems
• Could be simple, complex, or involved but solvable	• Are extremely complex, involved, and near impossible to solve
• Could be academic or real-world	• Are real-world
• Are static and constant or consistent	• Are dynamic and always changing or evolving
• Have stakes dependent on the scenario or situation	• Have high stakes because of the scenario or situation
• Have a well-defined and stable problem statement with clear boundaries, guidelines, rules, or steps to follow	• Lack a clear or common form, format, formula, or final solution; no clear boundaries, guidelines, rules, or steps to follow
• Have a definite stopping point; the experience ends when the solution is achieved or reached successfully	• Have no end or stopping point. The experience ends when ideas or resources are exhausted or the solution is good enough (for the moment).
• Have solutions that can be tested and tried	• Have solutions judged as good or bad, better or worse, or good enough or not good enough
• Have solutions that can be evaluated as correct or incorrect and true or false	• Have no specific categories, classifications, or criteria; every problem is unique to its context
• Can be categorized as a type of problem that can be solved in a similar way or with a specific set of processes and skills	• Are such that every attempt is a one-shot operation
• Come with a complete yet limited set of alternative solutions	• Have no finite set of solutions or template to address the problem
• Could have more than one symptom or solution	• Have multiple symptoms or could be symptoms of other problems
• Have a problem and solution agreed on by all those impacted or involved	• Feature no agreement about the problem or solution by those impacted or involved
• Can afford the problem solvers to be correct or incorrect. Negative consequences, impacts, and setbacks can be addressed or fixed.	• Cannot afford the problem solvers to be incorrect; negative consequences, impact, and setbacks could make the problem worse
• Can be addressed or assigned at any DOK level	• Are exclusive to a DOK 4 teaching and learning experience

these are the real-world problems and projects "that plague our cities and our world and touch each and every one of us" (p. 10). At some point, students will encounter an impossible or wicked issue, situation, or task that will not only test the depth and extent of their learning but will try their ingenuity and tax their perseverance. That's why these problems and projects are worth addressing.

DOK 4 teaching and learning experiences will prepare our students and provide them with the personal expertise they need to address a wicked problem or accomplish an impossible project effectively and perhaps even successfully. However, teachers should not be required to plan or provide a DOK 4 teaching and learning experience with every unit or lesson. Students should also not be required to demonstrate their learning at a DOK 4 level unless the standard's learning intention demands this. Treat and view DOK 4 teaching and learning experiences as an opportunity to enrich and extend students' learning, not as a goal or expectation. Use DOK 4 teaching and learning experiences to encourage students to recognize and realize how they could develop their education, experience, and endowments into personal expertise. This will make teaching and learning for Depth of Knowledge academically rigorous, socially and emotionally supportive, and student responsive.

Summary

We need to understand how the DOK levels can be used to plan and provide teaching and learning experiences that are academically rigorous, socially and emotionally supportive, and student responsive. A DOK 1 teaching and learning experience requires students to acquire and develop the foundational knowledge and functional understanding they need to succeed in a specific subject. A DOK 2 teaching and learning experience challenges students to comprehend and communicate how they can apply the content knowledge accurately to answer questions, address problems, accomplish tasks, or analyze ideas and information. DOK 3 teaching and learning experiences engage students to analyze how and why they could use the content knowledge as evidence to examine and explain answers, actions, analyses, alternatives, or arguments—their own or those made by others. DOK 4 teaching and learning experiences encourage students to explore and explain with examples and evidence how they could understand and use the content knowledge deep within a subject area, among texts and topics, across the curriculum, or beyond the classroom. Each of these DOK teaching and learning experiences differs in its level of rigor. However, each level serves an important purpose and role in the delivery of teachers' instruction and the development of students' learning.

Understanding Depth of Knowledge

Either on your own or as part of a teacher team, reflect on and respond to the following questions.

- How could you use the DOK levels to develop and deliver teaching and learning experiences that are academically rigorous, socially and emotionally supportive, and student responsive?

- How could you develop and deliver DOK 1 teaching and learning experiences that focus on knowledge acquisition?

- How could you develop and deliver DOK 2 teaching and learning experiences that target knowledge application?

- How could you develop and deliver DOK 3 teaching and learning experiences that engage students in knowledge analysis?

- How could you develop and deliver DOK 4 teaching and learning experiences that encourage knowledge augmentation?

CHAPTER THREE

How Can DOK Teaching and Learning Experiences Be Developed and Delivered?

In chapter 2 (page 27), we learned how teaching and learning for Depth of Knowledge support rigorous teaching and learning both academically and socially and emotionally. We also learned how each of the DOK levels describes the different level of rigor students can experience. However, how does a standard's learning intention define the rigor of a DOK teaching and learning experience? How do a standard's learning targets establish the goals and benchmarks for student performance? How can we evaluate students' level of Depth of Knowledge using a variety of assessments? What is the difference between teaching and testing, and teaching and learning for Depth of Knowledge? What role does the curriculum have in a DOK teaching and learning experience?

To answer these questions, this chapter aims to provide information on how to plan and provide DOK teaching and learning experiences. It explains how professional learning communities (PLCs) can use Depth of Knowledge to address the four critical questions posed by Rick and Rebecca DuFour (2012) that drive mission, vision, values, and goals of the PLC at Work® process. The chapter concludes with reflection questions to allow you to assess your understanding of Depth of Knowledge to this point.

How to Plan and Provide DOK Teaching and Learning Experiences

Planning and providing DOK teaching and learning experiences involve the following steps.

- Starting with the standards to set the learning targets of activities and assessments and establish the criteria for successful performance

- Surveying students' strengths to determine the delivery and intensity of the instruction

- Structuring teaching and learning as a pathway to proficiency and a progression of performance that leads to and beyond the standards' learning intention or goal target

- Supplementing, supporting, and stretching the teaching and learning experience using the texts and tasks provided by the curriculum

Figure 3.1 uses a single DOK block as a visual representation of a DOK teaching and learning experience. Within the frame of the DOK block are the benchmarks (standards), measures (assessment), methods (instruction), manner (learning), and materials (curriculum) used to plan and provide a DOK teaching and learning experience. Use this visual as a guide and map when developing and delivering DOK teaching and learning experiences for your students. However, keep in mind that the delivery and intensity of the DOK teaching and learning experience will always depend on the demand of the standards and the strengths of the student.

Planning and providing a DOK teaching and learning experience address the four critical questions that guide the professional learning communities (PLC) process for increasing student achievement, teacher effectiveness, and overall school performance (DuFour, DuFour, Eaker, Many, & Mattos, 2016).

1. **What do we want our students to learn?** This is defined by the DOK level of the standard being addressed or assessed.

2. **How will we know if each student has learned it?** This is determined by the activities and assessments that address the standard over a range of DOK levels.

3. **How will we respond when some students don't learn it?** This decides the delivery and intensity of the instruction.

4. **How can we extend and enrich the learning for students who have learned?** This depends upon both the demand of the standard and the strengths of the student.

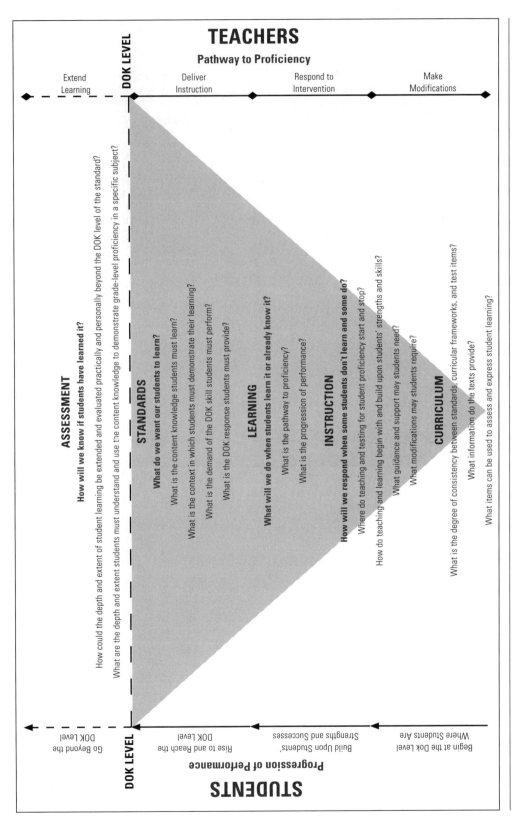

Figure 3.1: How to plan and provide DOK teaching and learning experiences.

This is how Depth of Knowledge complements and supports PLCs. Teacher and leadership teams can use the four critical questions of a PLC to plan and provide a DOK teaching and learning experience. PLCs can also use the DOK levels to translate course or grade-level goals into more specific unit plans and develop effective, consistent lesson plans (DuFour et al., 2016).

DOK and Standards

The demands of grade-level or content-area standards set the proficiency goals and expectations of a DOK teaching and learning experience. Its learning intention sets the ceiling of assessment—the deepest level at which test items will demand students to demonstrate learning. It also establishes the range of DOK levels at which activities and assessments could engage and evaluate students along the pathway to proficiency and progression of performance.

The DOK level of the learning intention answers the PLC question, "What do we want students to learn?" (DuFour et al., 2016). It identifies the complexity of content knowledge that students must learn at a given grade level. It also informs the depth and extent to which students must demonstrate their learning resulting from a teaching and learning experience. The standard's demand drives decisions regarding the delivery and intensity of the instruction. It also serves as the benchmark for determining the depth and extent of students' strengths.

To plan and provide a DOK teaching and learning experience, the standard's learning intention must be deconstructed to determine the Depth of Knowledge demanded and to designate its DOK level. It then needs to be reconstructed into a DOK *learning target* that specifies the mental processing—or DOK skill—students must perform. (This process will be explained further in chapters 5–7.) According to Ron Berger, Leah Rugen, and Libby Woodfin (2014), learning targets "translate [academic] standards into learning goals for lessons, projects, units, and courses, and are written in student-friendly language that is concrete and understandable" (p. 14). Figure 3.2 shows the difference between traditional learning targets and DOK learning targets that specify the DOK skill students must perform. The boldfaced phrase in the learning target emphasizes the DOK skill students must perform. Including the DOK skill makes the goal and expectation of a learning target both specific and measurable.

Figure 3.3 (page 55) shows how to use a standard's DOK learning targets to plot the pathway to proficiency and progression of performance in a DOK teaching and learning experience.

TRADITIONAL LEARNING TARGET	DOK LEARNING TARGET
I can explain why addition and subtraction strategies work, using place value and the properties of operations. (CCRS.Math-Content.2.NBT.B.9)	I can **use complex reasoning supported by evidence** to explain why the following addition and subtraction strategies work. • Place value (DOK 3) • The properties of operations (DOK 3)
I can explain how the use of text structure contributes to the author's purpose. (TEKS.ELA.4.10.B)	I can **use complex reasoning supported by evidence** to explain how the use of text structure contributes to the author's purpose. (DOK 3)
I can explain the difference between solids, liquids, and gases in terms of density, using the particle theory of matter. (Ontario.Science.8.ULS.3.4)	I can **apply knowledge, concepts, and skills** to explain the difference between solids, liquids, and gases in terms of density, using the particle theory of matter. (DOK 2)
I can explain how the perspectives of people in the present shape interpretations of the past. (C3 .D2.His.7.9–12)	I can **use extended reasoning supported by expertise** to explain how the perspectives of people in the present shape interpretations of the past. (DOK 4)
I can explain the differences and similarities between the word structures (derivation, prefixes, suffixes, and so on) in the target language and my own. (AERO.4.1.G5.c)	I can **apply knowledge, concepts, and skills** to explain the differences and similarities between the following word structures in the target language and my own. • Derivation (DOK 2) • Prefixes (DOK 2) • Suffixes (DOK 2)
I can explain how the method of display, the location, and the experience of interacting with an artwork influence how it is perceived. (NCAS.VA:Re.7.1.7a)	I can **use complex reasoning supported by evidence** to explain how the following influence the perception and value of an artwork. • The method of display (DOK 3) • The location (DOK 3) • The experience of interacting with the art (DOK 3)

Figure 3.2: The difference between traditional and DOK learning targets.

continued →

TRADITIONAL LEARNING TARGET	DOK LEARNING TARGET
I can explain how responses to music are informed by the structure, the use of the elements of music, and context (such as social and cultural). (NCAS.MU:Re7.2.4)	I can **apply knowledge, concepts, or skills** to explain how responses to music are informed by the following. • The structure (DOK 2) • The use of the elements of music (DOK 2) • The context (social and cultural) (DOK 2)
I can explain how body systems interact with one another during physical activity. (S3.M14.8)	I can **apply knowledge, concepts, or skills** to explain how body systems interact with one another during physical activity. (DOK 2)
I can explain the difference between civil law and criminal law. (ACHCK064)	I can **apply knowledge, concepts, or skills** to explain the difference between civil law and criminal law. (DOK 2)
I can explain the reasons for the rise and decline of early Singapore (Temasek) as a port-of-call across time. (Singapore MOE .History.Lower Secondary.1.2)	I can **use complex reasoning supported by evidence** to explain the reasons for the rise and decline of early Singapore (Temasek) as a port-of-call across time. (DOK 3)

Each of these DOK learning targets establishes the goals and expectations for activities and assessments that address a standard's learning intention. Some examples follow.

- The DOK learning goal target reconstructs the learning intention of the standard verbatim into an *I can* statement that specifies the mental processing students must perform to demonstrate proficiency or perform successfully.

- The DOK foundational targets identify the grade-level foundational knowledge (for example, factual and vocabulary) and functional understanding (for example, conceptual and procedural) students must develop to achieve the standard's DOK learning goal target.

- The DOK prerequisite targets itemize the essential or fundamental knowledge and skills that should have been taught and learned in a prior learning experience or a previous grade level or course of study.

- The EDOK developmental targets address and assess the individualized goals and expectations for students who receive and require specialized

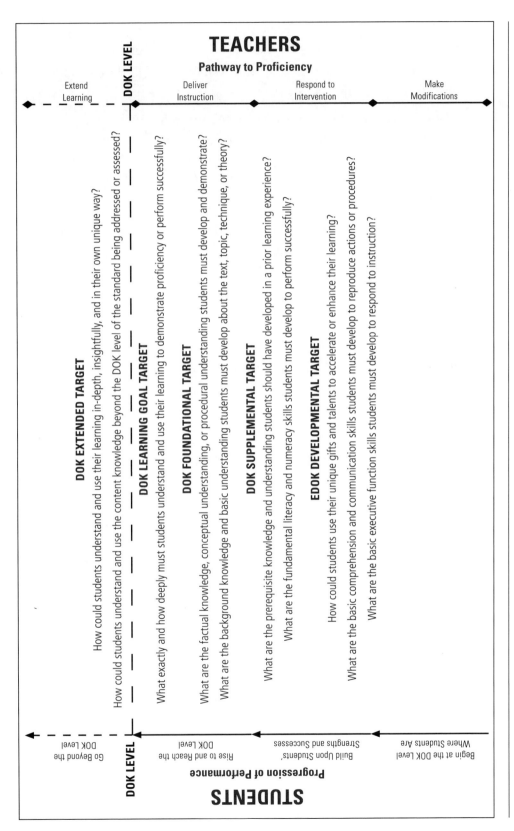

Figure 3.3: How to use DOK learning targets for standards-based learning.

services and support to achieve and surpass grade-level goals and expectations. These are based on the Extended DOK levels that H. Gary Cook developed for alternative assessments (2005, 2007). (We'll examine these further in chapter 4, page 67.)

- The DOK extended target prompts and encourages students to demonstrate their learning beyond the goals and expectations of a standard's learning intention.

DOK and Assessment

Assessing for Depth of Knowledge addresses the PLC question, "How will we know if students have learned it?" (DuFour et al., 2016). Figure 3.4 shows how DOK teaching and learning experiences use a variety of assessments to gauge students' strengths against the demand of the standard.

Each assessment serves a unique purpose in the evaluation of students' Depth of Knowledge. Some examples of assessment follow.

- The DOK summative assessment evaluates whether students can demonstrate their learning successfully at or up to the DOK ceiling of assessment set by the standard's learning intention at the end of an instructional unit, grade level, or course of study.

- The DOK interim assessments track students' progress toward demonstrating their learning at the DOK level demanded at certain intervals (for example, quarter and semester midterms).

- The DOK formative assessments help individual students realize what they need to succeed and recognize the DOK level at which they can demonstrate their learning. Student performance on these assessments reflects the depth and extent of their strengths.

- The DOK preassessment assesses individuals' and groups of students' levels of Depth of Knowledge at the start of a DOK teaching and learning experience and compares results with performance on interim or summative assessments.

- The DOK diagnostic assessments measure individual students' developmental skills and monitor their progress toward achieving individual goals.

- The DOK authentic assessments encourage and evaluate students' ability to demonstrate their learning practically and personally.

Figure 3.4: How to assess for Depth of Knowledge.

Student performance on these assessments drives decisions regarding the delivery and intensity of the instruction.

A standard's DOK learning targets can set the goals and expectations for assessments—especially if the test item prompts students to choose a response (for example, multiple choice, fill in the blank, matching, true or false, yes or no, agree or disagree). DOK learning targets can also be rephrased as success criteria statements that specify the demand of the response students must provide for activities, items, and tasks that are open-ended or subjective (such as short answers or essays).

Figure 3.5 shows DOK learning targets rephrased as DOK success criteria. DOK success criteria begin with the introductory phrase "Students must" to indicate the measure for successful performance for all students. Success criteria phrases in boldface emphasize the DOK response students must provide for activities and assessments that address the learning target. The DOK learning targets state what exactly and how deeply students must understand and use the learning to demonstrate proficiency or perform successfully. The DOK success criteria specify what exactly and how deeply students must respond to the activities, items, or tasks that address or assess the learning target. Finally, the demand of the DOK skill in the learning targets dictates the type of DOK response students must provide. For example, if the DOK learning target is a DOK 2 because it challenges students to apply knowledge, concepts, and skills, then students must establish and explain with examples for the activities, items, or tasks that address or assess the target at its DOK level.

The DOK success criteria make the expectations for student performance explicit and easy to evaluate. They also communicate the performance measures in a format and language that are clear and comprehensible to students. Students understand much more clearly what is required of them when an activity or assessment demands they *answer correctly, establish and explain with examples, examine and explain with evidence,* or *explore and explain with examples and evidence.*

DOK and Instruction

Instruction for Depth of Knowledge focuses on the following two areas: (1) assessing for student proficiency and (2) learning for student competency.

Teaching for Depth of Knowledge employs a tiered approach to measure and monitor student proficiency. The DOK levels serve as formative tiered benchmarks that check and confirm understanding. The instruction starts and stops with the standard, which sets the benchmarks for grade-level proficiency in a specific subject. If students

WHAT IS THE DOK LEARNING TARGET FOR THE ACADEMIC STANDARD?	WHAT ARE THE DOK SUCCESS CRITERIA FOR THE ACTIVITY OR ASSESSMENT?
I can **use complex reasoning supported by evidence** to explain why addition and subtraction strategies work by using the following. • Place value (DOK 3) • The properties of operations (DOK 3)	Students must **examine and explain with evidence** why addition and subtraction strategies work by using the following. • Place value (DOK 3) • The properties of operations (DOK 3)
I can **use complex reasoning supported by evidence** to explain how the use of text structure contributes to the author's purpose. (DOK 3)	Students must **examine and explain with evidence** how the use of text structure contributes to the author's purpose. (DOK 3)
I can **apply knowledge, concepts, and skills** to explain the difference between solids, liquids, and gases in terms of density, using the particle theory of matter. (DOK 2)	Students must **establish and explain with examples** what the difference is between solids, liquids, and gases in terms of density, using the particle theory of matter. (DOK 2)
I can **use extended reasoning supported by expertise** to explain how the perspectives of people in the present shape interpretations of the past. (DOK 4)	Students must **explore and explain with examples and evidence** over an extended period how the perspectives of people in the present shape interpretations of the past. (DOK 4)
I can **apply knowledge, concepts, and skills** to explain the differences and similarities between the following word structures in the target language and my own. • Derivation (DOK 2) • Prefixes (DOK 2) • Suffixes (DOK 2)	Students must **establish and explain with examples** the differences and similarities between the following word structures in the target language and their own. • Derivation (DOK 2) • Prefixes (DOK 2) • Suffixes (DOK 2)
I can **use complex reasoning supported by evidence** to explain how the following influence the perception and value of a work of art. The method of display (DOK 3) The location (DOK 3) The experience (DOK 3)	Students must **examine and explain with evidence** how the following influence the perception and value of a work of art. The method of display (DOK 3) The location (DOK 3) The experience (DOK 3)

Figure 3.5: DOK learning targets and DOK success criteria.

continued →

WHAT IS THE DOK LEARNING TARGET FOR THE ACADEMIC STANDARD?	WHAT ARE THE DOK SUCCESS CRITERIA FOR THE ACTIVITY OR ASSESSMENT?
I can **apply knowledge, concepts, and skills** to explain how responses to music are informed by the following. • The structure (DOK 2) • The use of the elements of music (DOK 2) • The context (social and cultural) (DOK 2)	Students must **establish and explain with examples** how responses to music are informed by the following. • The structure (DOK 2) • The use of the elements of music (DOK 2) • The context (social and cultural) (DOK 2)
I can **apply knowledge, concepts, and skills** to explain how body systems interact with one another during physical activity. (DOK 2)	Students must **establish and explain with examples** how body systems interact with one another during physical activity. (DOK 2)
I can **apply knowledge, concepts, or skills** to explain the difference between civil law and criminal law.	Students must **establish and explain with examples** what the difference is between civil law and criminal law.
I can **use complex reasoning supported by evidence** to explain the reasons for the rise and decline of early Singapore (Temasek) as a port-of-call across time.	Students must **examine and explain with evidence** what the reasons were for the rise and decline of early Singapore (Temasek) as a port-of-call across time.

struggle to demonstrate their learning at the DOK level demanded, the teacher tiers the instruction to the level where a student can perform successfully. The teacher then guides and supports students by delivering grade-level instruction, responding to intervention when necessary, or making modifications if needed. Teaching and testing for Depth of Knowledge stop once students demonstrate their learning proficiently and consistently at the DOK level demanded by the standard. However, teaching and learning for Depth of Knowledge guide and support students to understand and use their learning over a range of DOK levels leading to and beyond the standard. This makes teaching for DOK both standards-based and student-centered.

However, tiering instruction for Depth of Knowledge may not necessarily involve reducing the demand of the DOK teaching and learning experience. If a student can understand and use the learning at the level of Depth of Knowledge demanded by the standard's learning intention or target, then we should tier the instruction beyond the DOK level—or the DOK bar—set by the standard. Extending the teaching and learning experience beyond the DOK level of the standard will address and assess both the authenticity and sophistication of students' Depth of Knowledge.

Think of teaching for Depth of Knowledge like an obstacle course. The standard's learning intention is the finish line. The students are the competitors who must navigate through the activities and tasks of the course to reach the finish line. These activities and tasks—or obstacles—can vary in their demand. Some may be simple; others, complex or involved. The teacher is the coach who teaches and trains the students how to use and improve their unique strengths and skills to reach the finish line—or, in this case, to achieve the standard's learning intention or goal target successfully in their own time and to the best of their abilities. Once they achieve the standard's learning intention—or reach the finish line—the experience ends for the students because they have completed the course (figuratively and literally).

Teaching for Depth of Knowledge also addresses the PLC question, "How will we respond when individual students do not learn?" (DuFour et al., 2016). The teacher tiers the delivery and intensity of their instruction based on both the demand of the standard and the strengths of the student individually and collectively. The teacher also differentiates and individualizes instruction to assist and augment student learning. This makes teaching for Depth of Knowledge not only academically rigorous but also socially and emotionally supportive and student responsive.

DOK and Learning

As with teacher instruction, all roads for student learning lead to the level of Depth of Knowledge demanded by the standards. The pathway to proficiency steers students toward achieving the standard at its DOK level. The progression of performance guides and supports students to understand and use their learning over a range of DOK levels leading to the level of Depth of Knowledge the standard demands. This approach also makes DOK teaching and learning experiences both proficiency based and competency based. Students are guided and supported to draw on and develop their strengths and skills as they progress at their own pace toward achieving the grade-level goals and expectations set by a grade level or content-area standard's learning intention.

However, learning for Depth of Knowledge is not just about achieving grade-level goals and expectations to demonstrate proficiency. It inspires students to recognize their strengths and realize how they can build on them to achieve and surpass goals and expectations—be it the standards' expectations or their own. That's how the DOK blocks can be used to encourage students as well as educate and evaluate them. The pathway to proficiency shows students how they can develop their learning over a range of DOK levels to achieve and surpass the goals and expectations the standards set. The progression of performance guides students through developing their education, experiences, and endowments into personal expertise. All students, regardless of their capability or level of learning, should be guided, supported, and encouraged to rise to, reach, and go beyond the level of Depth of Knowledge the learning intention or target demands.

This is how learning for Depth of Knowledge addresses the PLC question, "How can we extend and enrich the learning for students who have learned it?" (DuFour et al., 2016). Each DOK level provides students a different and deeper opportunity to understand and use their learning. Teachers can use the DOK blocks to plan and provide teaching and learning experiences that will not only surpass the level of Depth of Knowledge the standards demand but also encourage students to understand and use their learning in deeper and more dynamic ways.

DOK and Curriculum

The curriculum provides the resources for teachers to teach and students to learn a specific subject at a given grade level. According to Richard Cash (2017), a rigorous curriculum should strengthen, support, and stretch each student "to grow intellectually, through engaging and challenging activities, to a point where the learner is self-directed, autonomous, and able to contribute successfully to society" (p. 28). The texts in the curriculum provide the content knowledge students must learn. Its activities and assessments vary in the depth and extent to which they demand students to demonstrate their learning.

The curriculum provides the examples and evidence educators can use to strengthen and support the responses to all four of the PLC critical questions (DuFour et al., 2016). However, you may need to adjust or modify the activities, items, or tasks to do the following.

- Address and assess the demand of the standard.

- Supplement and support the delivery and intensity of the instruction.

- Strengthen and stretch the depth and extent of students' learning.

Look at the sample mathematics activity in figure 3.6. The standard's DOK learning target and success criteria are a DOK 3 because they engage students to use complex reasoning supported by evidence to examine and explain why addition and subtraction strategies such as place value and the properties of operations work. The mathematics items from the curriculum, however, are a DOK 2 because they challenge students to apply knowledge, concepts, and skills to determine the unknown whole number in an addition or subtraction equation relating three whole numbers. To address and assess the demand of the standard, the teacher will need to deepen the delivery and intensity of their instruction and stretch the depth and extent to which the items demand

DOK LEARNING TARGET	DOK SUCCESS CRITERIA
I can use complex reasoning supported by evidence to explain why addition and subtraction strategies work using the following. • Place value (DOK 3) • The properties of operations (DOK 3)	Students must examine and explain with evidence why the following addition and subtraction strategies work. • Place value (DOK 3) • The properties of operations (DOK 3)
1) ___ +24 = 32 32 – ___ = 24	2) 68 – ___ = 31 ___ + 31 = 68
3) 46 – 30 = ___ 30 + ___ = 46	4) 59 – 27 = ___ 27 + ___ = 59
5) ___ + 24= 52 52 – ___ = 24	6) 93 – ___ = 26 26 + ___ = 93
7) 37 – 11 = ___ ___ + 11= 37	8) 81 – 26 = ___ 26 + ___ = 81
9) 29 + ___ = 73 73 – ___ = 29	10) 58 + ___ = 74 74 – ___ = 58

Figure 3.6: Sample mathematics activity with DOK learning target and success criteria.

students demonstrate their learning. (We will go into greater detail regarding how to designate DOK levels in chapter 6, page 101.)

With academic disciplines such as literature and the arts, the texts assigned or presented in class provide the examples and evidence students must understand and use to strengthen and support the DOK response to curricular activities, items, or tasks. For example, the DOK learning goal target "I can use complex reasoning supported by evidence to explain how the use of text structure contributes to the author's purpose" establishes the depth and extent to which students must understand and use their learning to demonstrate proficiency in fourth-grade English language arts and literature. The literary and informational texts students read in class provide the ideas and information—or evidence—they must examine and explain to strengthen and support their responses to curricular activities, items, and tasks that address and assess the DOK learning target. The texts change with each DOK teaching and learning experience that addresses and assesses the standard's DOK learning goal target.

To understand the role of the curriculum, think of teaching and learning for Depth of Knowledge as making music. The standard decides the song that the teacher must produce and that the students must perform. The curriculum provides instruments the teacher and students must play. However, the instruments may need to be tuned to ensure the teachers and students play the song at the proper pitch—or rather, deliver their teaching and demonstrate their learning at the level of Depth of Knowledge demanded by the standard's learning intention or target. The goals and expectations for demonstrating grade-level proficiency established by the standards cannot and should not be altered. They are the benchmark for assessment and instruction. However, the curriculum can be adjusted or differentiated so students can achieve and surpass the goals and expectations set by the standards and the students themselves. When it comes to the curriculum in a DOK teaching and learning experience, it's like Eric Clapton sings: "It's in the way that you use it" (Clapton & Robertson, 1986).

Summary

We need to understand how a standard's learning intention defines the demand of a DOK teaching and learning experience. We also need to deconstruct the standard's learning intention and reconstruct it into the DOK learning targets students must achieve to demonstrate proficiency, competency, and mastery. Teaching and testing for Depth of Knowledge start and stop with the standards. However, teaching and learning for Depth of Knowledge tier to the DOK level where students can perform successfully and build upon their strengths, skills, and successes so they can rise to, reach, and go beyond the level of Depth of Knowledge demanded by the standard. The curriculum provides the resources teachers can use to support instruction. Students respond to the activities, items, and tasks to showcase the depth and extent of their learning. However, the DOK level of a teaching and learning experience depends on the demand of the standard, the delivery and intensity of the instruction, and the strengths of the student.

Understanding Depth of Knowledge

Either on your own or as part of a teacher team, reflect on and respond to the following questions.

- How could you use Depth of Knowledge to align with the PLC process?

- How does the level of Depth of Knowledge demanded by your standards define exactly what students must learn and how deeply they must demonstrate their learning?

- How do your assessments measure and monitor the different levels of Depth of Knowledge that your students can use to demonstrate their learning?

- How could the DOK levels help you respond when some students struggle and some succeed in their learning?

- How could you use the DOK levels as a means for extending and enriching learning for all students?

- How could you use the DOK levels to encourage a growth mindset for learning with your students?

- How could you adjust or modify your curriculum to address and assess the demand of the standard, to strengthen and supplement the delivery and intensity of your instruction, or to strengthen and stretch the depth and extent of your students' learning?

CHAPTER FOUR

How Could the DOK Levels Serve as a Multitiered System of Supports?

In chapter 3 (page 49), we learned that DOK teaching and learning experiences are both standards-based and student-centered. We learned how Depth of Knowledge addresses the four critical questions that drive and guide the PLC process for increasing student achievement, teacher effectiveness, and overall school performance. We also learned what role standards, assessment, instruction, learning, and curricula play in a DOK teaching and learning experience. However, how might we plan and provide DOK teaching and learning experiences that tier instruction based on demand of the standard and the strengths of the student? How could the DOK levels be transformed into a multitiered system of supports—or MTSS—for delivering instruction, responding to intervention, extending learning, and making modifications for students who receive and require specialized services and supports to achieve and surpass grade-level goals and expectations?

To answer these questions, this chapter examines how the DOK levels could serve as a multitiered system of supports. It investigates the concept of response to intervention (RTI), specifically looking at the RTI at Work model and inverted pyramid (Buffum et al., 2018). It also explains how Depth of Knowledge could supplement this multitiered system of supports. The chapter delves into the complexities of using DOK with tiered intervention, extension, and modification efforts, providing a model from which educators can use DOK to enable high levels of learning for all students. The chapter concludes with reflection questions to allow you to assess your understanding of Depth of Knowledge to this point.

How to Tier DOK Teaching and Learning Experiences

Tiering a DOK teaching and learning experience involves the following.

- Delivering grade-level instruction to all students so they can demonstrate proficiency or perform successfully in a specific subject at a particular point of their education

- Providing preventive, supportive, and remedial interventions that respond to and support students achieving and surpassing the proficiency expectations set by the standards and the personal expectations they have set for themselves

- Making modifications for students with exceptional needs so they can develop basic competency and accomplish academic and developmental goals

- Offering opportunities for extension and enrichment of student learning that will engage and encourage students to demonstrate their learning beyond the level of Depth of Knowledge the standards demand

Figure 4.1 features the DOK blocks with the RTI at Work model developed by Buffum and colleagues (2018). Their representation transforms the RTI process into an instructional methodology that responds to the academic and socioemotional needs of each individual student. RTI aims to allow every student the support, resources, and time needed to learn at high levels (Buffum et al., 2018). To do this, it utilizes three levels or *tiers*: (1) Tier 1, which represents core instruction; (2) Tier 2, which represents supplemental interventions, and (3) Tier 3, which represents intensive supports for students who need them most. These tiers are represented within the inverted RTI at Work pyramid, with Tier 1 comprising the largest segment at the top of the pyramid, Tier 2 in the middle, and Tier 3 at the bottom or pointy end of the pyramid. The point itself represents the student, such that all efforts and interventions are focused on a single point—the individual student. This model enables schools, educators, and teacher teams to "view these tiers [not] as a pathway to traditional special education but instead as an ongoing process to dig deeper into students' individual needs" (Buffum et al., 2018, p. 19).

Placing the inverted RTI pyramid within a DOK block provides both a strategy and a system that tier the delivery and intensity of the DOK teaching and learning

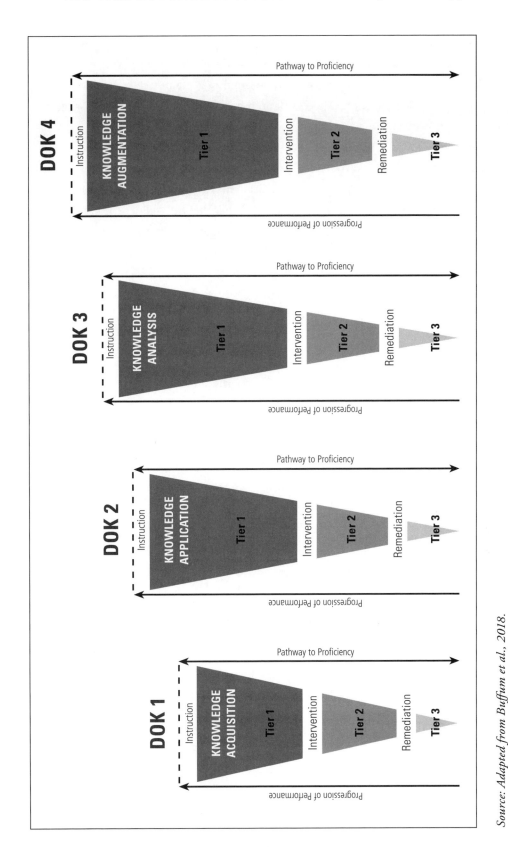

Source: Adapted from Buffum et al., 2018.

Figure 4.1: How to use the DOK levels as a multitiered system of supports.

experience based on the demands of the standard and the strengths of the student. Each DOK level utilizes the RTI process to guide and support students in demonstrating their learning at the level of Depth of Knowledge an academic standard's learning intention or target demands. This follows Barbara Blackburn's (2013) concept of rigor, which involves "creating an environment in which each student is expected to learn at high levels, and each is supported so he or she can learn at high levels, and each student demonstrates learning at high levels" (p. 19). The teacher tiers their instruction to address and assess deficiencies and gaps in students' learning. However, instead of focusing on what students *don't know* or *can't do*, the teacher differentiates and individualizes instruction to determine the level of Depth of Knowledge students individually or as a whole class can perform successfully. This makes the RTI process and interaction between the teacher and student more positive, or more socially and emotionally supportive. The teacher tiers to and builds on the students' strengths and successes so they can rise to, reach, and go beyond the level of Depth of Knowledge demanded by the standard's learning intention or target (the DOK bar of the DOK block). That's how Depth of Knowledge makes the RTI process student responsive.

Figure 4.2 uses a single DOK block to show how the RTI at Work process tiers the pathway to proficiency and the progression of performance of a DOK teaching and learning experience. The DOK bar serves as the benchmark for standardization and the goal of RTI, which is "to ensure all students learn at high levels—grade level or better each year" (Buffum et al., 2018, p. 21). The inverted pyramid within the DOK block details the delivery and intensity of instruction students could receive or require depending on the DOK level of their strengths and skills. Any activity or assessment that prompts and encourages students to demonstrate their learning beyond the standard's learning intention is addressed and assessed as an extension of student learning. That's why it's placed above the DOK bar and the inverted RTI pyramid within the DOK block.

The following sections will go into more detail about how to tier DOK teaching and learning experiences for (1) intervention, (2) extension, and (3) modification.

DOK and Intervention

The RTI at Work pyramid divides the DOK block into three tiers that differentiate instruction and individualize learning based on both the demand of the standard and the success of the students. Figure 4.3 (page 72) shows the RTI process within an individual DOK teaching and learning experience. The tiers within the DOK block indicate and inform the delivery and intensity of instruction. Each tier addresses and assesses the DOK learning targets derived from the standard's learning intention.

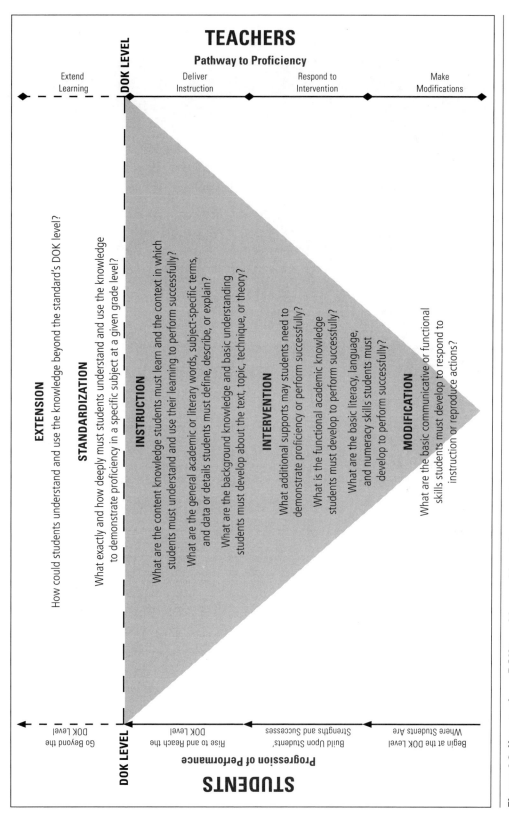

Figure 4.2: How to tier a DOK teaching and learning experience.

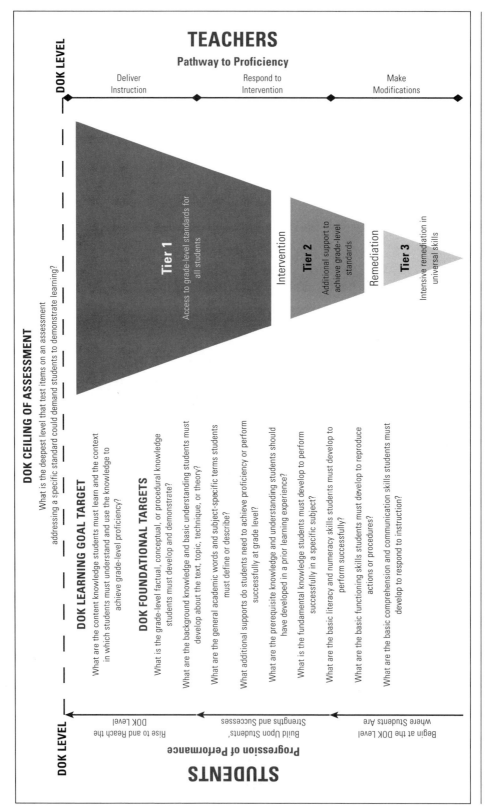

Figure 4.3: The RTI process within an individual DOK teaching and learning experience.

However, the delivery and intensity of instruction depend on both the demand of the standard and the strengths of the student.

Tier 1 of a DOK teaching and learning experience educates and expects students to understand and use the learning at the level of Depth of Knowledge demanded by the current grade level's academic standard. The instructional focus and purpose of Tier 1 are "to provide all students access to essential grade-level curriculum and effective initial teaching" (Buffum et al., 2018, p. 20). The DOK learning target and success criteria reconstructed from the standard's learning intention establish the goals and expectations for demonstrating grade-level proficiency or performing successfully in a specific subject.

Tier 1 interventions in a DOK teaching and learning experience are preventive. The instructional focus and purpose of intervention are to recognize and respond to where students are in their learning and in relation to the DOK level of the grade-level standard. This determines the delivery and intensity of instruction. For example, if students struggle to demonstrate their learning at the DOK level demanded by the standard, the teacher must tier the instruction to the DOK level that the students are at and guide and support them in reaching the level of Depth of Knowledge demanded by the standard's learning intention or target.

In Tier 2 of a DOK teaching and learning experience, students are provided "with the additional time and support needed to master the specific skills, knowledge, and behaviors identified at Tier 1 to be absolutely essential for a student's future success" (Buffum et al., 2018, p. 21). This extended time and supplemental support can be provided during or beyond the regularly scheduled class period. Students also may be grouped with peers who share similar strengths or experience similar struggles. Once students demonstrate they can achieve the DOK learning target successfully, the teacher builds upon that success to guide and support students toward demonstrating their learning proficiently and consistently.

Interventions provided in Tier 3 of a DOK teaching and learning experience are more individualized and intense. These interventions are more remedial, focusing on the fundamental or prior knowledge students should have learned in a previous grade or in a correlating course of study. They support students in developing what Buffum and colleagues (2018) call *universal skills*—the critical skills "that enable a student to comprehend instruction, access information, demonstrate understanding, and behaviorally function in a school setting" (p. 22). The universal skills include functional skills in literacy, language, and numeracy. Interventions are provided by the classroom teacher and educators with specialized credentials or training (for example, reading specialist, mathematics interventionist, special education teacher, or language learner teacher) through small group or one-to-one instruction.

The DOK learning targets addressed and assessed in Tier 1 and Tier 2 are recon-structed from the current grade-level standard. The DOK learning targets in Tier 3 address and assess the fundamental content knowledge covered in previous grade levels. DOK levels can vary based on the demand of the standards and the strengths of the student. For example, the second-grade mathematics standard that demands students explain why addition and subtraction strategies work is a DOK 3. Its DOK level is deeper than some correlating mathematics standards from higher grade levels. However, it identifies and informs the fundamental or prior knowledge students need to succeed; that's why it is addressed and assessed in a Tier 3 intervention.

The tiers of the inverted RTI pyramid within the DOK block are not meant to label students or place them permanently at a specific level of learning. They supplement and support grade-level teaching and learning, rather than substituting or supplant-ing them. Students also should not be limited to or prevented from demonstrating their learning outside a specific RTI tier in a DOK teaching and learning experience. The purpose of RTI in a DOK teaching and learning experience is to ensure all stu-dents—no matter the tier at which they can perform successfully—receive the rigor-ous instruction necessary and responsive interventions they need to succeed. Students should also be permitted and prompted to move through the tiers toward and beyond achieving the standard's learning intention or goal target.

Responding to intervention with Depth of Knowledge involves tiering the teaching to the DOK level at which students can understand and use their learning successfully. If the student proves they can perform successfully, then the instruction expands or extends to deeper levels until the student shows signs of struggle. The level at which the student struggles is where they need intensive intervention. This is a positive approach to addressing gaps. Instead of determining or even presuming what students don't know or can't do or produce, the intervention is based and built on what students do know or can do or produce.

DOK and Extension

Educators can also use the DOK levels to plan and provide teaching and learning experiences that extend beyond the level of Depth of Knowledge demanded by a stan-dard's learning intention. One way to do this is to expand the instructional focus and purpose of its learning intention. For example, consider the following standard:

> "Determine an author's point of view or purpose in a text and explain how it
> is conveyed in the text." (CCSS.ELA-Literacy.RI.6.6; NGA & CCSSO, 2010b)

This English language arts standard is a DOK 3. It engages students to use complex reasoning supported by evidence from a single text to determine and explain an author's point of view or purpose. If we expand the instructional focus and purpose to encourage students to explore and explain, with examples and evidence, the point of view or purpose of two or more authors or two or more texts that address the same topic, the teaching and learning experience becomes a DOK 4.

Another way to extend learning is to address a standard that takes the DOK teaching and learning experience in a different direction. For example, consider the following standard.

> "Compare and contrast one author's presentation of events with that of another (e.g., a memoir written by and a biography on the same person)." (CCSS.ELA-Literacy.RI.6.9; NGA & CCSSO, 2010c)

The level of Depth of Knowledge demanded by this ELA standard's learning intention is a DOK 4. Students are encouraged to distinguish with examples and evidence two presentations of the same topic. It shifts the instructional focus and purpose of the DOK teaching and learning experience from assessing the point of view and purpose of a text to analyzing how two or more texts address similar themes or topics and comparing the approaches the texts or authors take.

Connecting the content knowledge across the curriculum also extends the DOK teaching and learning experience. For example, consider the following example:

> "Evaluate the relevancy and utility of a historical source based on information such as maker, date, place of origin, intended audience, and purpose." (C3.D2.His.13.6–8; National Council for the Social Studies, 2013)

The learning intention of this history standard is a DOK 3 because it engages students to use complex reasoning supported by evidence. However, it extends the DOK teaching and learning experience because it engages students to understand and use their content knowledge from different subjects—in this case, social studies.

A standard from a subsequent grade level could also extend the learning. Consider, for example, the following.

- "Determine two or more central ideas in a text and analyze their development over the course of the text; provide an objective summary of the text." (CCSS.ELA-Literacy.RI.7.6; NGA & CCSSO, 2010b)

- "Determine an author's point of view or purpose in a text and analyze how the author acknowledges and responds to conflicting evidence or viewpoints." (CCSS.ELA-Literacy.RI.8.6; NGA & CCSSO, 2010b)

- "Determine an author's point of view or purpose in a text and analyze how an author uses rhetoric to advance that point of view or purpose." (CCSS.ELA-Literacy.RI.9–10.6; NGA & CCSSO, 2010b)

- "Determine an author's point of view or purpose in a text in which the rhetoric is particularly effective, analyzing how style and content contribute to the power, persuasiveness or beauty of the text." (CCSS .ELA-Literacy.RI.11–12.6; NGA & CCSSO, 2010b)

The learning intention of all these ELA standards is a DOK 3—the same as the targeted grade-level standard. However, not only do these standards expand the instructional focus and purpose, but they also engage students to achieve the learning intention and targets from higher grade levels. These learning intentions can support academic acceleration, which Peter Merrotsy (2008) says is "the study of new material that is typically taught at a higher grade level than the one in which the child is currently enrolled" (p. 4).

Addressing standards from higher grade levels is one way to extend student learning. However, extension of learning is not synonymous with exceeding the standards. Buffum and colleagues (2018) define extension as "when students are stretched beyond essential grade-level curriculum or levels of proficiency" (p. 28). Students who extend their learning beyond the DOK level of a specific standard should not be described as exceeding the standard. *Exceeding* does not describe the demand of a DOK teaching and learning experience.

DOK and Modifications

Some students have diverse or unique needs that require specialized services and support for them to achieve and surpass grade-level goals and expectations. These students are taught the same academic standards as their peers. However, activities and assessments are modified so these students can demonstrate proficiency or perform successfully to the best of their abilities or potential. Examples of such students include those with special needs, English learners, and students identified as gifted and talented (GT) or twice-exceptional (2E).

The Extended DOK Stages—or EDOKs—developed by H. Gary Cook (2005, 2007) are a DOK model used to categorize and compare the cognitive demand of academic standards and developmental assessments for students who require specialized services and support, such as in alternative assessments given to special education students or language proficiency assessments for English learners. Cook split DOK 1 into three distinct levels—or stages—that demand students demonstrate their ability to respond (EDOK 1), reproduce (EDOK 2), and recall (DOK 1). This expanded Webb's DOK levels from four to six. The EDOKs are no longer used in alignment studies of alternative assessments. However, they could be used to categorize and confirm the demand of student-specific cognitive and language developmental goals and expectations set in the individual education plans (IEPs) for exceptional students or Individualized Learning Plans (ILPs) for English or second language learners.

Figure 4.4 (page 78) represents the DOK levels and EDOK stages as DOK blocks. It shows how both DOK models can be used together as an MTSS method and model that inform how to modify activities and assessments. Webb's DOK levels designate the demand of grade-level goals and expectations established by the learning intention of academic standards, activities, and assessments. The EDOK stages categorize and confirm the demand of the specific developmental goals and expectations for a student with limited comprehension and communication skills. For exceptional learners, the EDOKs categorize and confirm the demand of the annual academic goals and short-term objectives of a student's individualized education plan or IEP. With English learners, the EDOKs categorize and confirm the demand of language development objectives listed under the level descriptors of language proficiency standards. The EDOKs are superimposed over the DOK levels to make the DOK teaching and learning experience even more student-centered. That's why the EDOK blocks are represented with dashed lines.

Though both EDOKs address and assist students with developing basic comprehension and communication skills, the intent of the modifications differs. The EDOKs for exceptional students emphasize cognitive development. The EDOKs for English learners focus on language development. When making modifications, consider to whom the "E" in EDOK pertains and serves.

The DOK levels can also be expanded for students identified who demonstrate high ability, motivation, and potential. Figure 4.5 (page 79) modifies the DOK blocks into a multitiered system of support for students identified as gifted and talented. I call these *GDOK blocks*—the "G" standing for "gifted" or "going further," which is what the GDOKs do. They accelerate (GDOK 1) or enrich (GDOK 2) the delivery and intensity of grade-level instruction for students who demonstrate high ability, motivation, or potential. Those are the types of services GT students could receive or require. The depth and extent of the GDOK block is relative to the level of Depth of Knowledge demanded by the grade-level academic standard, activity, or assessment. For example, if the level of Depth of Knowledge demanded by a learning intention is a DOK 2, a GDOK 1 accelerates the DOK teaching and learning experience horizontally by challenging a GT student to understand and use their learning at a higher grade level

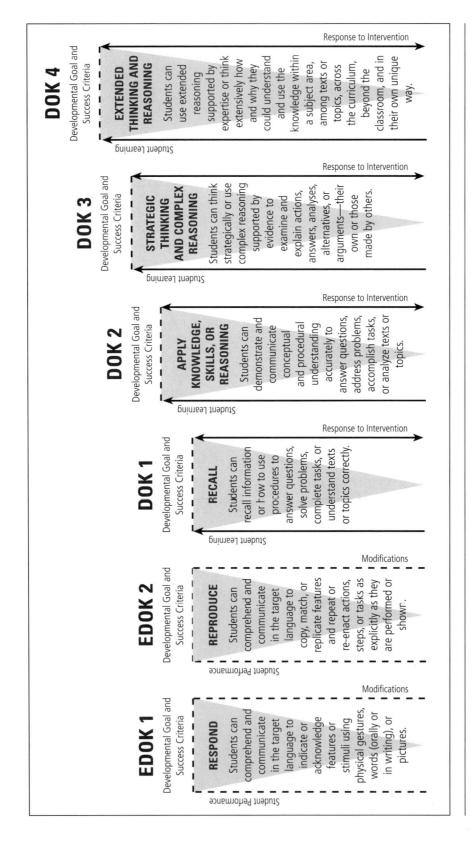

Figure 4.4: DOK levels of learning and EDOK stages of development.

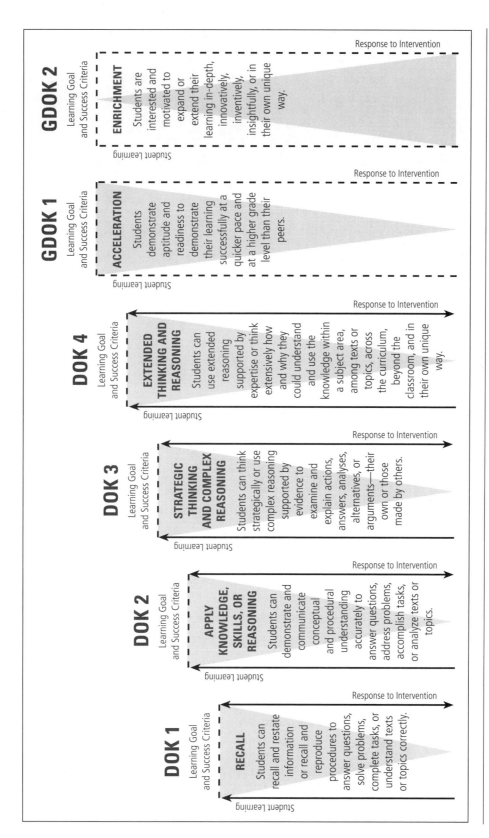

Figure 4.5: DOK levels and GDOK services as an MTSS for gifted and talented students.

(for example, a fifth-grade student understanding and using the learning at an eighth-grade, high school, or college level). Examples of GDOK 1 strategies include curriculum compacting and grade skipping. The GDOK 2 enriches a DOK teaching and learning experience for GT students by connecting the content to students' personal interests or piquing students' curiosity to delve deeper or go further with their learning. Examples of GDOK 2 include offering independent study, using study contracts, or creating learning centers within or beyond the classroom that either address and augment the content or cater to the students' strengths and interests.

The GDOK blocks are extremely individualized and personalized, addressing and assessing both students' strengths and their personal interests to augment their learning. That's why the RTI pyramid within the GDOK blocks is upright instead of inverted—to accelerate and enrich the delivery and intensity of instruction based on the demand of the standard and the strengths and interests of the individual student.

The GDOKs also ensure GT students have the opportunity to understand and use their learning at all DOK levels, not just the deeper ones. Students who demonstrate high ability, motivation, or potential should not always or only be required to understand and use their learning at the deepest DOK levels. Conversely, these students should also not be disallowed to or dissuaded from demonstrating their learning at reduced or simpler DOK levels. This complements and supports the philosophy and practice of the Schoolwide Enrichment Model developed by Joseph Renzulli and Sally Reis (2014), which promotes that all students should have the opportunity to accelerate and enrich their learning. However, the delivery and intensity of the acceleration and enrichment depend on the unique aptitude and interests—or strengths—of the individual student.

Both the EDOKs and GDOKS could be used to address and support the unique strengths and needs of dual-identified students. For example, the EDOKs for cognitive and language development can be used to modify activities and assessments for English learners who also receive and require special education services. The GDOKs can be used with the EDOKs for cognitive and language development to accelerate or enrich a DOK teaching and learning experience for 2E students or ELL students identified as gifted and talented, respectfully. Both the cognitive and language development EDOKs and the GDOKS could also be used to address and assess the unique strengths and needs of an English learner who is identified as gifted and talented but faces learning or developmental challenges.

Neither the EDOKs nor the GDOKs serve as another level of Depth of Knowledge at which students must demonstrate their learning. Like the DOK levels, they serve as categories, specifying the different and deeper ways students with specific and unique strengths and needs can be supported or stimulated to achieve and surpass proficiency and personal goals and expectations. They also provide an extra layer of support for students to demonstrate proficiency or perform successfully to the best of their ability and potential. They are adaptable and flexible so teachers can modify the delivery and intensity of their instruction based on the demand of the standard and the strengths of the student. This is why the EDOKs and GDOK blocks are represented as dashed lines. You can overlay or merge them with any of the DOK blocks to make the DOK teaching and learning experience academically rigorous, socially and emotionally supportive, and responsive to the unique strengths and needs of a specific student.

Summary

We need to understand how DOK teaching and learning experiences can be tiered based on the demand of the standard and the success of the students. We also need to understand how the DOK levels can be used as a multitiered system of supports to deliver instruction, respond to intervention, extend learning, and make modifications. Each DOK level utilizes the RTI process to guide and support students in demonstrating their learning at the level demanded by a standard's learning intention or target. The tiers within the DOK levels determine the delivery and intensity of instruction students receive and require. Extended DOK teaching and learning experiences can demand that students demonstrate their learning beyond the DOK or grade level of a standard's learning intention. The EDOK stages address, assess, and assist exceptional learners or English learners in developing the basic comprehension and communication skills they need to succeed. The GDOKs accelerate and enrich DOK teaching and learning experiences for students who demonstrate high ability, motivation, or potential. Like the RTI tiers, the EDOKs and GDOKs supplement and support students who receive and require specialized services and supports to achieve and surpass proficiency and personal goals and expectations.

Understanding Depth of Knowledge

Either on your own or as part of a teacher team, reflect on and respond to the following questions.

- How could you use the DOK levels to deliver grade-level instruction for all students?

- How could you use the DOK levels to provide preventive interventions for struggling students in Tier 1?

- How could you use the DOK levels to provide supplemental interventions for struggling students in Tier 2?

- How could you use the DOK levels to provide intensive interventions for struggling students in Tier 3?

- How could you use the DOK levels to extend student learning beyond the cognitive demand of a standard's learning intention?

- How could you use the EDOK stages to make modifications for students who receive and require special education services and support?

- How could you use the EDOK stages to make modifications for English learners who are acquiring and developing fluency in the school's target language?

- How could you use the GDOK stages to accelerate or enrich the DOK teaching and learning experience for gifted and talented students who demonstrate high ability, motivation, or potential?

PART II

USING

DEPTH

of

KNOWLEDGE

CHAPTER FIVE

How to Deconstruct Learning Intentions for Depth of Knowledge

In chapter 4 (page 67), we learned how to tier the delivery and intensity of a DOK teaching and learning experience based on the demand of the standard and the strengths of the student. However, how does the performance expectation state the instructional focus by identifying what exactly students must learn? How does the context inform the instructional purpose by specifying how deeply students must complete the performance expectation? What if an academic standard's learning intention has more than one cognitive action verb or objective?

To answer these questions, this chapter will break down the process of deconstructing a standard's learning intention to determine the Depth of Knowledge demanded. You will discover how to identify and isolate important aspects of the learning intention, including the performance expectation and context. You will also recognize which part of a standard's learning intention determines the level of Depth of Knowledge demanded. You will also realize a standard's learning intention could contain multiple objectives that determine its overall DOK level. The chapter concludes by presenting a reproducible chart to help you begin deconstructing your own learning intentions and standards.

How to Deconstruct a Learning Intention to Determine the Depth of Knowledge Demanded

Determining the Depth of Knowledge demanded involves deconstructing a standard's learning intention to do the following.

- Confirm the performance expectation.

- Clarify the context.

- Check the phrasing of the learning intention.

Figure 5.1 shows how to deconstruct a standard's learning intention to its individual parts. This is the DOK chart—a visual aid and tool we will use over the next couple chapters to deconstruct the learning intention of our standards, activities, and assessments, and to designate their DOK levels. The verb of the learning intention indicates the type of thinking and indicates the cognitive action students will demonstrate. The noun or noun phrase identifies the content knowledge students will learn. It also states the instructional focus. The words and phrases that complete the learning intention detail the context in which students must demonstrate their learning. They also inform the scope and stipulations of the instructional purpose. The complexity of both the instructional focus and purpose determines the Depth of Knowledge demanded by the standard's learning intention.

TYPE OF THINKING	DEPTH OF KNOWLEDGE	
What is the cognitive action?	What is the instructional focus?	What is the instructional purpose?
To + verb	The noun or noun phrase that states what exactly students must learn	The words and phrases that specify how deeply students must demonstrate their learning
Performance Expectation		Context

Figure 5.1: DOK chart for deconstructing learning intentions.

Confirm the Performance Expectation

The first step in deconstructing a learning intention for Depth of Knowledge is to confirm its performance expectation. The performance expectation "states what a learner is expected to do and/or produce to be considered competent" (Mager, 1997, p. 46). It consists of a verb that indicates the cognitive action students must perform, and a noun or noun phrase that names the content knowledge students will learn. For example, consider the following mathematics standard.

> "Simplify numerical expressions that do not involve exponents, including up to two levels of grouping." (TEKS.MATH.5.4[F]; Texas Education Agency, 2011)

The learning intention of this mathematics standard starts with the cognitive action verb *to simplify*. This is the type of thinking students must demonstrate. The noun phrase "numerical expressions" names the content knowledge students will be thinking about—or in this case, simplifying. It's also the instructional focus. Both describe the performance expectation.

Figure 5.2 shows how to use the DOK chart to deconstruct the performance expectation of this mathematics standard into its individual components. Writing *to simplify* in its infinitive form affirms this is the cognitive action and type of thinking students will perform. It will also be helpful when reconstructing the learning intention into a DOK learning target. (We'll learn more about this in chapter 7, page 117.) The noun phrase *numerical expressions* identifies not only what the instructional focus is but also what exactly students must learn. That's why it's listed under the column Depth of Knowledge.

TYPE OF THINKING	DEPTH OF KNOWLEDGE
What is the cognitive action?	What is the instructional focus?
To simplify	Numerical expressions
Performance Expectation	

Figure 5.2: How to enter the performance expectation in the DOK chart.

The instructional focus specifies the content area in which students will demonstrate their thinking. According to Hess (2018), "Thinking and accessing information stored in long-term memory is domain specific, not simply generic mental processing" (p. 37). For example, analyzing informational or text-dependent subjects such as literature or history demands a different set of mental processing skills than analyzing within a subject that's procedural (such as mathematics) or performance-based (such as art, music, or physical education). The instructional focus confirms the mental processing—or DOK skill—students must perform to complete the performance expectation in that specific subject area. Figure 5.3 (page 88) shows the range of DOK skills a learning intention could demand students perform when they are expected to analyze content knowledge in a specific subject. The specific DOK skill will designate the DOK level of the academic standard, activity, or assessment.

TYPE OF THINKING	DEPTH OF KNOWLEDGE	
What is the cognitive action?	What is the instructional focus? (content area)	What is the DOK skill?
To analyze	Proportional relationships (mathematics)	Recall how to Apply knowledge, concepts, and skills Think strategically Think extensively
	Points of view (literature and language arts)	Recall information Use information and basic reasoning Use complex reasoning supported by evidence Use extended reasoning supported by expertise
	Geoscience data (science)	Recall how to Apply knowledge, concepts, and skills Think strategically Think extensively
	Wars between Persia and the Greek city-states (history)	Recall information Use information and basic reasoning Use complex reasoning supported by evidence Use extended reasoning supported by expertise
	Public policies (civics)	Recall information Use information and basic reasoning Use complex reasoning supported by evidence Use extended reasoning supported by expertise
	Cultural and environmental characteristics (geography)	Recall information Use information and basic reasoning Use complex reasoning supported by evidence Use extended reasoning supported by expertise

To analyze	Components of visual imagery (visual arts)	Recall how to Apply knowledge, concepts, and skills Think strategically Think extensively
	Elements of music (fine arts)	Recall information Use information and basic reasoning Use complex reasoning supported by evidence Use extended reasoning supported by expertise
	Target cultures (world language)	Recall how to Apply knowledge, concepts, and skills Think strategically Think extensively
	Food choices (health and physical education)	Recall information Use information and basic reasoning Use complex reasoning supported by evidence Use extended reasoning supported by expertise
Performance Expectations		Cognitive Demand

Figure 5.3: DOK chart showing how the instructional focus specifies the DOK skills students must perform.

The instructional focus also distinguishes the DOK skill demanded by learning intentions that expect students to demonstrate the same type of thinking. Consider the performance expectations in figure 5.4 (page 90). They both expect students to identify. However, ideas and themes are a more complex concept than literary elements. This instructional focus also demands students perform a deeper DOK skill.

Clarify the Context

The context of a learning intention details the depth and extent to which students will demonstrate their learning. It also informs the instructional purpose—the scope and stipulations for students to complete the performance expectation. Figure 5.5 (page 90) shows which words and phrases clarify the depth and context in which students must simplify numerical expressions. The scope and stipulations are itemized—or what George A. Miller (1956) describes as *chunked*—to make the scope and stipulations of the instructional purpose explicit and easier to read or review.

TYPE OF THINKING	DEPTH OF KNOWLEDGE	
What is the cognitive action?	What is the instructional focus?	What is the DOK skill?
To identify	Literary elements	Recall information
	Ideas and themes	Use complex reasoning supported by evidence
Performance Expectations		Cognitive Demand

Figure 5.4: Sample DOK chart distinguishing performance expectations and cognitive demands for a standard with the same type of thinking.

TYPE OF THINKING	DEPTH OF KNOWLEDGE	
What is the cognitive action?	What is the instructional focus?	What is the instructional purpose?
To simplify	Numerical expressions	That do not involve exponents Including up to two levels of grouping
Performance Expectations		Context

Figure 5.5: Sample DOK chart identifying the instructional purpose in certain contexts.

The context also clarifies the DOK skill students perform. Consider the learning intentions in figure 5.6. Notice how the context specifies the DOK skill demanded when students are expected to analyze certain content knowledge in a specific subject.

The context also distinguishes the cognitive demand of learning intentions with similar performance expectations. Consider the learning intentions in figure 5.7 (page 93). Notice how the context clarifies the depth and extent to which students must identify literary elements. The context also determines the cognitive demand of the DOK skill students must perform.

TYPE OF THINKING	DEPTH OF KNOWLEDGE		
What is the cognitive action?	What is the instructional focus?	What is the instructional purpose?	What is the DOK skill?
To analyze	Proportional relationships	Use them to solve the following: • Mathematical problems • Real-world problems	Think strategically
	Points of view	How differences of the following create such effects as suspense or humor: • Characters • Reader or audience	Use complex reasoning supported by evidence
	Geoscience data	To make the claim that one change to Earth's surface can create feedbacks that cause changes to other Earth systems	Think strategically
	Wars between Persia and the Greek city-states	• The major events • The reasons why the Persians failed to conquer the Aegean region	Use information and basic reasoning
	Public policies	The following in multiple settings: • Purposes • Implementation • Consequences	Use complex reasoning supported by evidence
	Cultural and environmental characteristics	The ways in which they vary among different regions of the world	Use information and basic reasoning

Figure 5.6: Sample DOK chart clarifying the context and cognitive demand of performance expectations.

continued →

TYPE OF THINKING	DEPTH OF KNOWLEDGE		
What is the cognitive action?	What is the instructional focus?	What is the instructional purpose?	What is the DOK skill?
To analyze	Components of visual imagery	How they convey messages	Apply knowledge, concepts, and skills
	Elements of music	How they relate to the following: • Style • Mood	Use information and basic reasoning
	Target cultures	Formal and informal patterns of the following: • Behavior • Cultural practices	Use information and basic reasoning
	Food choices	Impact relative to the following: • Physical activity • Youth sports • Personal health	Use complex reasoning supported by evidence
Performance Expectation		Context	Cognitive Demand

The context also clarifies the complexity and rigor of learning intentions with cognitive action verbs considered higher-order thinking. The cognitive action verb in the following examples, *to create*, is categorized as the highest level of thinking students can demonstrate, according to Bloom's revised taxonomy (Anderson & Krathwohl, 2001).

- "Create a chronological sequence of multiple events." (C3.D2.His.K–2; National Council for the Social Studies, 2013)

- "Create and use a chronological sequence of related events to compare developments that happened at the same time." (C3.D2.His.3–5; National Council for the Social Studies, 2013)

- "Create and use a chronological sequence of events to analyze connections among events and developments in broader historical contexts." (C3.D2.His.6–8; National Council for the Social Studies, 2013)

TYPE OF THINKING	DEPTH OF KNOWLEDGE		
What is the cognitive action?	What is the instructional focus?	What is the instructional purpose?	What is the DOK skill?
To identify	Literary elements	In a text	Recall information
		How they interact with each other	Use information and basic reasoning
		Their impact on other aspects of the text (for example, craft and structure)	Use complex reasoning supported by evidence
		Of two or more texts written within the same genre Their impact on other aspects of the text	Use extended reasoning supported by expertise
Performance Expectations		Context	Cognitive Demand

Figure 5.7: Sample DOK chart clarifying different contexts for a standard with similar performance expectations.

- "Create and use a chronological sequence of events to evaluate how historical events and developments were shaped by unique circumstances of time and place as well as broader historical contexts." (C3.D2.His .9–12; National Council for the Social Studies, 2013)

While the cognitive action verb, *to create*, determines the type of thinking required in the preceding standards, the words and phrases that complete these learning intentions identify both what students must create and how deeply. These words and phrases determine the cognitive demand of the mental processing—or DOK skill—students must perform and the true complexity and rigor of the learning intention. Figure 5.8 (page 94) shows where these learning intentions would be placed in the Create row of Hess's Cognitive Rigor Matrix (see figure 1.2, page 20). Notice all these learning intentions are coded a BLOOM's 6. However, the DOK level differs based on what exactly and how deeply each learning intention demands students to create.

BLOOM'S REVISED TAXONOMY	WEBB'S DOK LEVELS			
	DOK 1	DOK 2	DOK 3	DOK 4
Create	Create a chronological sequence of multiple events. (BLOOM's 6, DOK 1)	Create and use a chronological sequence of related events to compare developments that happened at the same time. (BLOOM's 6, DOK 2)	Create and use a chronological sequence of events to analyze connections among events and developments in broader historical contexts. (BLOOM's 6, DOK 3)	Create and use a chronological sequence of events to evaluate how historical events and developments were shaped by unique circumstances of time and place as well as broader historical contexts. (BLOOM's 6, DOK 4)

Figure 5.8: How to use the Hess CRM to determine the cognitive rigor of learning intentions.

Check the Phrasing of the Learning Intention

Some learning intentions are phrased as a simple statement that features a single objective. However, many standards feature multiple objectives, as does, for example, the following.

> "Determine the meaning of words and phrases as they are used in a text, including figurative, connotative, and technical meanings; analyze the impact of a specific word choice on meaning and tone." (ELA-Literacy.RI.7.4; NGA & CCSSO, 2010b)

This English language arts learning intention features two cognitive action verbs: "to determine" and "to analyze." Each introduces a separate objective. Figure 5.9 shows how to use the DOK chart to deconstruct this standard's learning intention into its two discrete objectives.

Some learning intentions may be phrased as a single statement that features two or more objectives. For example, consider the following history standard.

> "Explain the causes of the U.S. Civil War and evaluate the importance of slavery as a principal cause of the conflict." (USE.Std.3A.5–12; National Center for History in the Schools, 1996)

TYPE OF THINKING	DEPTH OF KNOWLEDGE	
What is the cognitive action?	What is the instructional focus?	What is the instructional purpose?
To determine	The meaning of words and phrases	As they are used in a text, including the following: • Figurative meanings • Connotative meanings
To analyze	Word choice	Specific impact on the following: • Meaning • Tone
Performance Expectations		Context

Figure 5.9: Sample DOK chart for standards with multiple objectives.

The learning intention of this history standard features two objectives connected by the conjunction *and*. The objectives are distinct—they differ in their performance expectation and context. Figure 5.10 shows how to deconstruct this learning intention into its two objectives. Activities and assessments could address one or both objectives. However, students must complete both objectives to demonstrate grade-level proficiency.

TYPE OF THINKING	DEPTH OF KNOWLEDGE	
What is the cognitive action?	What is the instructional focus?	What is the instructional purpose?
To explain	The U.S. Civil War	The causes
To evaluate	Slavery	Its importance as a principal cause of the conflict
Performance Expectations		Context

Figure 5.10: Sample DOK chart for deconstructing compound objectives.

A learning intention that begins with two or more cognitive action verbs followed by the same instructional focus and purpose signals that students must perform multiple steps, such as in the following example.

"Identify and explain similarities and differences between basic word order language systems." (AERO.WL.4.1.G2; Project AERO, 2018)

The learning intention of this world language standard demands students perform two steps. First, they must identify similarities and differences in the basic word order of language systems. Then they must explain those similarities and differences. Figure 5.11 shows how to use the DOK chart to deconstruct this learning intention and specify the steps students must perform. Students must complete both steps—or objectives—to demonstrate grade-level proficiency.

TYPE OF THINKING	DEPTH OF KNOWLEDGE	
What is the cognitive action?	What is the instructional focus?	What is the instructional purpose?
To identify	Basic word order	Similarities and differences in language systems
To explain		
Performance Expectations		Context

Figure 5.11: Sample DOK chart for deconstructing standards that require multiple steps.

Some learning intentions feature a primary objective that describes the performance expectation followed by one or more objectives that detail the conditions of the context. Consider this example.

"Develop and use a model to describe the function of a cell as a whole and ways the parts of cells contribute to the function." (NGSS-MS-LS1–2; NGSS Lead States, 2013)

The performance expectation of this science standard demands students develop a scientific model. That's the primary objective. The objectives that follow the performance expectation are conditional objectives that inform the instructional purpose. They could be deconstructed to determine their cognitive demand; however, they are not separate or independent objectives students must complete. They clarify the context in which students must complete the performance expectation. Figure 5.12 shows how to deconstruct this science standard into its primary and conditional objectives.

Some learning intentions feature cognitive action verbs in different forms or tenses, as in the following example.

TYPE OF THINKING	DEPTH OF KNOWLEDGE	
What is the cognitive action?	What is the instructional focus?	What is the instructional purpose?
To develop	A scientific model	And use it to describe the following: The function of a cell Ways parts of cells contribute to the function
Performance Expectations		Context

Figure 5.12: Sample DOK chart for deconstructing a standard into primary and conditional objectives.

> "Find whole-number quotients of whole numbers with up to four-digit div-idends and two-digit divisors, using strategies based on place value, the properties of operations, and/or the relationship between multiplication and division." (MATH.CONTENT.5.NBT.B.6; NGA & CCSSO, 2010a)

This mathematics standard features two verbs. The verb *to find* introduces one objective. The verb *using* introduces another. That verb needs to be converted into its infinitive form to indicate it is a cognitive action that students must perform. Figure 5.13 (page 98) shows how to deconstruct the learning intention into these two discrete objectives. The verb *using* is rephrased in its infinitive form *to use* to indicate this is a cognitive action that students must perform.

Summary

Deconstructing learning intentions for Depth of Knowledge is a complex process. It demands that we go beyond identifying the key concepts and skills students must learn by circling verbs and underlining nouns. However, to make it easier, keep the following in mind.

- The verb that introduces the learning intention indicates the cognitive action students must perform. Once you identify that, isolate the verb and look at the words and phrases that follow it. Those words and phrases will determine the Depth of Knowledge demanded.

TYPE OF THINKING	DEPTH OF KNOWLEDGE	
What is the cognitive action?	What is the instructional focus?	What is the instructional purpose?
To find	Whole-number quotients	With up to four-digit dividends and two-digit divisors
To use	Strategies	Based on the following: • Place value • The properties of operations • The relationship between multiplication and division
Performance Expectations		Context

Figure 5.13: Sample DOK chart for standards with two objectives.

- Look for the noun or noun phrase that names the content knowledge students will think about or learn. That's the instructional purpose. Once you identify that, you confirm the performance expectation—namely, what exactly students must know and do or produce.

- All the words and phrases that follow the verb of the learning intention clarify the context in which students must complete the performance expectation. That's the instructional purpose. Itemize or chunk those words and phrases to make the conditions and criteria of the instructional purpose clear, comprehensible, and concise.

- If the learning intention features more than one verb, that means the standard demands students complete more than one objective. Isolate those verbs and go through the process of deconstructing the objectives.

- If the standard features two objectives connected by a conjunction or a comma, that indicates the learning intention features compound objectives. Both of those objectives need to be deconstructed.

- If a standard starts with two or more cognitive action verbs and has the same instructional focus and purpose, that means the learning intention is a multistep performance or process. Both of those objectives need to be deconstructed.

- The first objective in a standard's learning intention is the primary objective that describes the performance expectation. All the objectives that follow the performance expectation are conditional objectives that clarify the context and inform the instructional purpose.

- If a learning intention features a verb in a different form or tense, then that verb needs to be written in its infinitive form to indicate this is a cognitive action that students are expected to perform.

- Any cognitive action verb in a learning intention in any form or tense could introduce an objective that students must complete.

- Activities and assessments could address any objective within a standard's learning intention. However, students must complete all the objectives to demonstrate grade-level proficiency at the DOK level demanded.

Using Depth of Knowledge

Either on your own or as part of a teacher team, complete the following tasks.

Choose a learning intention from one of your grade-level or content-area academic standards, activities, or assessments. Use the DOK chart in the reproducible "DOK Chart for Deconstructing Learning Intentions" (page 100) to do the following.

1. Write the statement of the objective from your standards or curriculum in the row called Learning Intention. Don't rephrase it. Write it just as it's presented or printed.

2. Identify the verb that introduces the learning intention. Write it in the column that asks, "What is the cognitive action?" This is the type of thinking students must demonstrate. Put it aside and don't be concerned with it anymore.

3. Look for the noun or noun phrase that identifies the content knowledge students will be thinking about and learning. List that under the column that asks, "What is the instructional focus?" Now you know the performance expectation.

4. Write the rest of the words and phrases that complete the learning intention in the column that asks, "What is the instructional purpose?" Now you know the instructional purpose.

5. If there are more verbs within the learning intention, write them in the column that asks, "What is the cognitive action?" Repeat the process for identifying the instructional focus and informing the instructional purpose. Now you know how many objectives are within the learning intention.

DOK Chart for Deconstructing Learning Intentions

Learning Intention:		
What is the cognitive action?	**What is the instructional focus?**	**What is the instructional purpose?**
Performance Expectations		Context

CHAPTER SIX

How to Designate the DOK Level a Task Demands

In chapter 5 (page 85), we learned how to deconstruct a learning intention to confirm the performance expectation and clarify the context in which students will demonstrate their learning. We learned that the instructional focus and purpose of a learning intention determine the level of Depth of Knowledge demanded. We also learned that we need to check the phrasing of the learning intention to identify how many objectives students must achieve. However, what designates the DOK level of an academic standard, activity, or assessment? How do the instructional focus and purpose determine the demand of the DOK task students must complete, the DOK skill students must perform, and the DOK response students must provide? If a learning intention features multiple objectives, which one designates the overall DOK level of the academic standard, curricular activity, or test item? Also, what if the cognitive demand of the instructional focus or purpose is unclear or questionable?

To answer these questions, this chapter discusses several important aspects of designating the DOK level of a learning intention. You will learn to determine the DOK task students must complete, the DOK skill students must perform, and the DOK response students must provide. You will also discover how to proceed if the learning intention has more than one objective, what to do if the DOK level is unclear, and how to use the DOK descriptors as a checks and balances system. The chapter concludes with a reproducible tool to help you determine the DOK level for your own learning intention.

How to Designate the DOK Level

You can designate the level of Depth of Knowledge demanded by an academic standard, activity, or assessment based on one or more of the following.

- The DOK task students must complete

- The DOK skill students must perform

- The DOK response students must provide

Figure 6.1 expands the DOK chart to include a section to confirm the cognitive demand of a learning intention. The columns in the Cognitive Demand section feature the DOK descriptors that define what exactly and how deeply students must understand and use their learning in the simplest and most specific terms. These DOK descriptors also help designate the level of Depth of Knowledge demanded according to the DOK levels.

TYPE OF THINKING	DEPTH OF KNOWLEDGE					
What is the cognitive action?	What is the instructional focus?	What is the instructional purpose?	What is the DOK task?	What is the DOK skill?	What is the DOK response?	What is the DOK level?
To + verb	Name of content knowledge	Conditions and criteria	Expectation of the activity or item students must complete	Specific mental processing students must perform	Extent of the response students must provide	DOK 1 DOK 2 DOK 3 DOK 4
Performance Expectations		Context	Cognitive Demand			

Figure 6.1: DOK chart for designating the DOK level.

Define the DOK Task

The DOK task defines what exactly and how deeply students must understand and use the learning to complete a curricular activity or test item successfully. Figure 6.2 features the DOK descriptors that define the different task demands at each DOK level. They describe what academic standards, activities, and assessments demand students know and do or produce.

The demand of the DOK task depends on "the complexity of both the content (e.g., interpreting literal versus figurative language) and the required task (e.g., solving

WHAT IS THE DOK LEVEL?	WHAT DOES THE DOK TASK DEMAND FROM STUDENTS?
DOK 1 (low)	Just the facts
	Just do it
DOK 2 (moderate)	Show and share or summarize
	Demonstrate and communicate
	Specify and explain
	Give examples and non-examples
DOK 3 (high)	Delve deeply
	Inquire and investigate
	Think critically or problem solve
	Think creatively
	Defend, justify, or refute with evidence
	Connect, confirm, conclude, consider, or critique
DOK 4 (extensive)	Go deep within a subject area
	Go among texts and topics
	Go across the curriculum
	Go beyond the classroom

Figure 6.2: DOK levels and the demand of DOK tasks.

routine versus non-routine problems)" (Hess et al., 2009a, p. 4). The DOK task descriptors describe the complexity in language that's clear and comprehensible—especially for students. Using these DOK task descriptors will help students recognize and realize what they must know and do or produce to demonstrate proficiency, perform successfully, or progress in their learning.

To define the demand of the DOK task, clarify the complexity of the content knowledge students must learn and confirm the conditions and criteria of the task students must complete. Then ask, "What exactly and how deeply must students know and do, produce, or provide to address the standard or accomplish the task?" Answer the question with one of the DOK task descriptors. The resulting response will determine the Depth of Knowledge demanded and designate the DOK level.

Determine the DOK Skill

The DOK skill specifies the mental processing students must perform. It is determined by "the depth of content understanding and scope of a learning activity, which manifests in the skills required to complete the task from inception to finale (e.g., planning, researching, drawing conclusions)" (Hess et al., 2010a, p. 4). Figure 6.3 shows the different DOK skills students could perform at each DOK level.

WHAT IS THE DOK LEVEL?	WHAT IS THE DOK SKILL STUDENTS MUST PERFORM?
DOK 1 (low)	Recall information Recall how to
DOK 2 (moderate)	Apply knowledge, concepts, and skills Use information and basic reasoning
DOK 3 (high)	Think strategically Use complex reasoning supported by evidence
DOK 4 (extensive)	Use extended reasoning supported by expertise Think extensively

Figure 6.3: DOK levels and the demand of DOK skills.

The DOK skill is also particular to the kind of knowledge students must think about or develop. Figure 6.4 features the different kinds of knowledge categorized by the knowledge dimension of Bloom's revised taxonomy developed by Anderson and Krathwohl (2001) and extended by John Walkup (2020). Notice how factual and procedural knowledge demands that students understand and use a specific set of DOK skills. With the other kinds of knowledge, the DOK skill demanded depends on the context in which students demonstrate their learning.

To determine the DOK skill students must perform, identify the content area in which students will demonstrate their thinking and classify the kind of knowledge the instructional focus expects students to develop. Then verify the scope and stipulations of the academic standard, activity, or assessment. That will specify the mental processing—or DOK skill—students must perform to demonstrate proficiency or perform successfully.

Decide the DOK Response

Another way to designate the DOK level demanded is to decide the DOK response students must provide. Figure 6.5 (page 106) shows the different and deeper ways each DOK level can demand students respond.

The DOK response dictates the success criteria for what exactly and how deeply students must respond. It also communicates the expectations for performance in a language and manner that are clear and easy to understand. It's easy for both educators

Knowledge dimension	What is the instructional focus?	What are the DOK skill and level?
Factual knowledge	Knowledge of terminology	DOK 1: Recall information
		DOK 2: Use information and basic reasoning
	Knowledge of specific details and elements	DOK 3: Use complex reasoning supported by evidence
		DOK 4: Use extended reasoning supported by expertise
Procedural knowledge	Knowledge of algorithms and formulas	DOK 1: Recall how to
		DOK 2: Apply knowledge, concepts, or skills
	Knowledge of methods and techniques	DOK 3: Think strategically
		DOK 4: Think extensively
	Knowledge of criteria	
Conceptual knowledge	Knowledge of categories and classifications	Depends on the context (instructional purpose)
	Knowledge of principles and generalizations	
	Knowledge of models, structures, and theories	
Metacognitive knowledge	Strategic knowledge	
	Conditional or contextual knowledge	
	Self-knowledge	
Relevance knowledge	Personal (immediate)	
	Personal (future)	
	Professional	
	Social	
	Academic or scholarly	
Communicative knowledge	Vocabulary	
	Writing	
	Speaking	
	Listening	

Sources: Adapted from Anderson & Krathwohl, 2001; Walkup, 2020.

Figure 6.4: Kinds of knowledge and their specific DOK skills.

WHAT IS THE DOK LEVEL?	WHAT IS THE DOK RESPONSE STUDENTS MUST PROVIDE?
DOK 1 (low)	Answer correctly
DOK 2 (moderate)	Establish and explain with examples
DOK 3 (high)	Examine and explain with evidence
DOK 4 (extensive)	Explore and explain with examples and evidence

Figure 6.5: DOK levels and the demand of DOK responses.

and students to recognize and realize whether an academic standard, activity, or assessment simply requires students to answer correctly or engages them to examine and explain with evidence.

We could decide the DOK response in two different ways. We could conclude the depth and extent to which an academic activity or assessment demands students respond. Alternatively, we could also determine the DOK level of an academic standard's learning intention and decide the depth and extent to which students must respond to the activities and assessments that address the standard.

How to Proceed If the Learning Intention Has More Than One Objective

If a learning intention features multiple objectives, then its most cognitively demanding objective designates the overall DOK level of the standard. For example, in figure 6.6, the first objective is a DOK 2 because it challenges students to establish and explain with examples (DOK response) how to apply knowledge, concepts, and skills (DOK skill) to determine the different meanings of words and phrases as they are used in a text. The second objective is a DOK 3 because it engages students to delve deeper (DOK task) to examine and explain with evidence (DOK response) the impact specific word choice has on meaning and tone. That's the DOK ceiling of assessment. It designates the overall DOK level of the learning intention a DOK 3.

With compound objectives, the second objective usually designates the overall DOK level of the learning intention. For example, in figure 6.7 (page 108), the second objective is a DOK 3 because it demands students inquire and investigate (DOK task) how they can use complex reasoning supported by evidence (DOK skill) to examine and explain (DOK response) slavery's role as a principal cause of the U.S. Civil War.

TYPE OF THINKING		DEPTH OF KNOWLEDGE				
What is the cognitive action?	What is the instructional focus?	What is the instructional purpose?	What is the DOK task?	What is the DOK skill?	What is the DOK response?	What is the DOK level?
To determine	The meaning of words and phrases	As they are used in a text, including the following: • Figurative meanings • Connotative meanings	Demonstrate and communicate	Apply knowledge, concepts, and skills	Establish and explain with examples	DOK 2 (moderate)
To analyze	Word choice	Its impact on the following: • Meaning • Tone	Delve deeper	Use complex reasoning supported by evidence	Examine and explain with evidence	DOK 3 (high)
Performance Expectations		Context			Cognitive Demand	

Figure 6.6: How to designate the DOK level for a learning intention with multiple objectives.

TYPE OF THINKING		DEPTH OF KNOWLEDGE				
What is the cognitive action?	What is the instructional focus?	What is the instructional purpose?	What is the DOK task?	What is the DOK skill?	What is the DOK response?	What is the DOK level?
To explain	The U.S. Civil War	The causes	Specify and explain	Use information and basic reasoning	Establish and explain with examples	DOK 2 (moderate)
To evaluate	Slavery	Its importance as a principal cause of the conflict	Inquire and investigate	Use complex information supported by evidence	Examine and explain with evidence	DOK 3 (high)
Performance Expectations		Context		Cognitive Demand		

Figure 6.7: How to designate DOK levels for learning intention with compound objectives.

Activities and assessments could address either of these objectives. However, the items and tasks must address the second objective to be deemed fully aligned to the standard.

The number of objectives in a standard's learning intention will not impact the overall DOK level of the standard, as in the following example.

> "Know relative sizes of measurement units within one system of units including km, m, cm; kg, g; lb, oz.; l, ml; hr, min, sec. Within a single system of measurement, express measurements in a larger unit in terms of a smaller unit. Record measurement equivalents in a two-column table."
> (MATH.CONTENT.4.MD.A.1; NGA & CCSSO, 2010a)

Figure 6.8 (page 110) shows how to use the DOK chart to deconstruct this mathematics standard, determine the Depth of Knowledge demanded by its three objectives, and designate their DOK levels. All three objectives are a DOK 1 because they require students to recall (DOK skill) *just the facts* (DOK task) and recall how to (DOK skill) *just do it* (DOK task) to answer correctly (DOK response). DOK 1 is the overall DOK level of the mathematics standard. Stacking or sequencing these objectives as steps will not deepen the overall DOK level. It's the requirement of the most cognitively demanding objective, not the number of objectives, that designates the overall DOK level of an academic standard, activity, or assessment. Since they are all a DOK 1, that's also the overall DOK level.

How to Proceed If the DOK Level Is Unclear

Sometimes the DOK level is unclear because the context of the instructional purpose is too broad or vague. Consider the following example.

> "Explain a proof of the Pythagorean Theorem and its converse." (MATH.CONTENT.HSF.BF.A.1.A; NGA & CCSSO, 2010a)

This learning intention of this mathematics standard seems to only require students to recall (DOK skill) just the facts (DOK task) to answer correctly (DOK response), which would designate it a DOK 1. However, an argument could be made that it challenges students to show and share or summarize (DOK task) how they can apply knowledge, concepts, and skills (DOK skill) to establish and explain with examples (DOK task) a proof of both the Pythagorean Theorem and its converse, which would designate the standard a DOK 2. Mathematical proofs engage students to use it to prove it (DOK task) by thinking strategically (DOK skill) to examine and explain with evidence (DOK response), which would designate the learning intention a DOK 3. So, what is the DOK level of this mathematics standard?

TYPE OF THINKING		DEPTH OF KNOWLEDGE				
What is the cognitive action?	What is the instructional focus?	What is the instructional purpose?	What is the DOK task?	What is the DOK skill?	What is the DOK response?	What is the DOK level?
To know	Measurement units	Relative sizes within one system of units, including the following: • km, m, cm • kg, g • lb, oz • l, ml • hr, min, sec	Just the facts	Recall information	Answer correctly	DOK 1 (low)
To express	Measurements	In a larger unit in terms of a smaller unit within a single system of measurement	Just do it	Recall how to	Answer correctly	DOK 1 (low)
To record	Measurement equivalents	In a two-column table	Just do it	Recall how to	Answer correctly	DOK 1 (low)
Performance		Context	Demand			

Figure 6.8: How to designate the DOK levels for a mathematics learning intention with multiple objectives.

According to Hess (2018), if the DOK level of the learning intention is unclear or questionable, it's acceptable and appropriate to designate it as a deeper DOK level. In fact, teachers should teach the academic standard, activity, or assessment at that deeper DOK level. They can adjust or modify the delivery and intensity of their instruction and the materials provided in the curriculum so students will demonstrate their learning at those deeper DOK levels. However, teaching and learning experiences should also provide students opportunities to demonstrate their learning over a range of DOK levels leading to and beyond the level demanded by the standard. This ensures that the DOK teaching and learning experience addresses and assesses student performance and progress fairly and formatively. It also provides teachers with the data and information they need to determine whether they must adjust or modify their instruction to assist or augment students' learning.

How to Use the DOK Descriptors as a Checks and Balances System

The DOK descriptors can be used as a checks and balances system for concluding the DOK level of academic standards, activities, and assessments. For example, if the activity or assessment is a DOK 2 because it demands students establish and explain with examples (DOK response), then we can conclude that the task will challenge students to show and share, demonstrate and communicate, specify and explain, or give examples and non-examples (DOK task) of how they can apply knowledge, concepts, and skills or use information and basic reasoning (DOK skill).

The DOK descriptors can also be used to check and balance the degree of alignment between academic standards, activities, and assessments. For example, if the academic standard is a DOK 2 because it demands students inquire and investigate (DOK task), then the activity or assessment must engage students to use complex reasoning (DOK skill) to examine and explain (DOK response) to be deemed fully aligned. If the activity or assessment only requires students to recall (DOK skill) just the facts or demonstrate how to just do it (DOK task) to answer correctly, then both would be rated insufficiently aligned to the demand of the standard.

Figure 6.9 (page 112) is a matrix for checking and balancing the DOK level of academic standards, activities, and assessments. I added a column titled *DOK It* to describe the goal and expectations at each DOK level in the simplest terms possible for us educators and our students to understand (for example, answer it, use it to explain it, use it to prove it, or go for it). These descriptors also make the goals and expectations of the DOK teaching and learning experience more concise, precise, and purposeful.

DOK TASK	DOK SKILL	DOK RESPONSE	DOK IT	DOK LEVEL
Just the facts Just do it	Recall information Recall how to	Answer correctly	Answer it	DOK 1 (low)
Show and share or summarize Demonstrate and communicate Specify and explain Give examples and non-examples	Apply knowledge, concepts, and skills Use information and basic reasoning	Establish and explain with examples	Use it to explain it	DOK 2 (moderate)
Delve deeply Inquire and investigate Think critically or problem solve Think creatively Defend, justify, or refute with evidence Connect, confirm, conclude, consider, or critique	Think strategically Use complex reasoning supported by evidence	Examine and explain with evidence	Use it to prove it	DOK 3 (high)
Go deep within a subject area Go among texts and topics Go across the curriculum Go beyond the classroom	Use extended reasoning supported by expertise Think extensively	Explore and explain with examples and evidence	Go for it	DOK 4 (extensive)

Figure 6.9: DOK checks and balances matrix.

To use the matrix to designate the DOK level demanded, first choose the DOK descriptor that best describes the demand of the academic standard, activity, or task. Use the descriptor that best matches how you view academic standards, activities, or assessments. For example, if you are a task-oriented person, use the DOK task descriptors to define the Depth of Knowledge demanded. If you are someone who considers the mental processing students must perform, use the DOK skill descriptors. If you base the demand on how students must respond, use the DOK response descriptor. To help your students understand the goal and expectations for each DOK level, use the DOK It descriptors. Check across the row to determine the Depth of Knowledge demanded and designate the DOK level.

The DOK checks and balances matrix also serves as a rubric for coding and comparing the level of Depth of Knowledge demanded by academic standards, activities, and assessment items. The criteria for DOK consistency depend on the following.

- If the demand of the standard, activity, or assessment's DOK descriptors matches across a row, it is fully aligned.

- If the activity or assessment's DOK descriptor is one row above the standard's, it is acceptably aligned.

- If the activity or assessment's DOK descriptor is two or more rows above the standard's, it is insufficiently aligned.

- If the activity or assessment's DOK descriptor is one or more rows above the standard's, it demands students go beyond the standard's learning intention.

The DOK checks and balances matrix should not be used as a teacher evaluation tool. Teachers should not be evaluated based on the level of Depth of Knowledge demanded by their instruction or assessments. They should also not be expected or required to teach and test only at the deeper DOK levels. Such an expectation and requirement is unfair and unreasonable. However, instructional leaders and coaches could also use the DOK checks and balances matrix as a resource to assist teachers in addressing and augmenting the level of Depth of Knowledge demanded by their curriculum, instruction, and assessments. For example, if a curricular activity requires students to answer correctly, the instructional leader or coach could use the DOK checks and balances matrix to show the teacher how they could deepen the DOK level by challenging students to establish and explain with examples (DOK response) how they applied the knowledge, concepts, and skills, or to use information and basic reasoning (DOK skill) to attain their response or result. This deepens the cognitive demand of the teaching and learning experience from a DOK 1 to a DOK 2.

When coaching teachers to develop and deliver DOK teaching and learning experiences, ask them to share how they view the demand of academic standards, activities, and assessments. Do they consider the demand of the task students must complete, the mental processing students must perform, or the response students must provide? Use the corresponding DOK descriptors to help them determine the level of Depth of Knowledge demanded by academic standards, activities, and assessments. Also, show them how they could use the DOK descriptors to develop, deliver, and deepen their DOK teaching and learning experiences.

Summary

The DOK descriptors are the deciding or driving factor for designating the DOK level of a learning intention. In fact, the DOK descriptor you use depends on how you look at academic standards, activities, or assessments.

- Do you consider the depth and extent to which the task demands students understand and use the content knowledge in a certain context? Use the descriptors of the DOK task.

- Do you consider the complexity of the mental processing students must perform and the kind of knowledge students must develop? Use the descriptors of the DOK skill.

- Do you consider the depth and extent to which students must address or respond to an activity, item, or task? Use the descriptors of the DOK response.

Any of the DOK descriptors will help you designate the DOK level demanded by an academic standard, activity, or assessment. Using them will also help you plan and provide DOK teaching and learning experiences that communicate the goals and expectations for successful student performance clearly.

Using Depth of Knowledge

Either on your own or as part of a teacher team, complete the following tasks.

Use the learning intention of the academic standard, activity, or assessment from chapter 5 (page 85) or choose another one. Use the reproducible "DOK Chart for Determining the Depth of Knowledge Demanded by a Learning Intention" (page 116) to do the following.

- Deconstruct the learning intention to confirm its performance expectation and clarify its context.

- Determine what exactly the instructional focus and purpose require students to understand and how deeply they demand students to use the content knowledge.

- Choose the DOK descriptor that best describes the demand of the DOK task students must complete, the DOK skill students must perform, or the DOK response students must provide.

- Designate the DOK level of the learning intention according to the DOK levels.

- Use the reproducible DOK chart on page 116 to check and balance the DOK level between academic standards and the activities or assessments that address its learning intention.

DOK Chart for Determining the Depth of Knowledge Demanded by a Learning Intention

LEARNING INTENTION							
Type of Thinking		Depth of Knowledge					
What is the cognitive action?	What is the instructional focus?	What is the instructional purpose?	What is the DOK task?	What is the DOK skill?	What is the DOK response?	What is the DOK level?	
Performance Expectations	Context				Cognitive Demand		

CHAPTER SEVEN

How to Construct DOK Learning Targets and Success Criteria

In chapter 6 (page 101), we learned how to designate the DOK level of a learning intention based on the demand of the DOK task, the DOK skill students must perform, and the DOK response students must provide. We also learned these DOK descriptors describe the cognitive demand of academic standards, activities, and assessments in the simplest terms. However, how could we reconstruct a standard's learning intention into a DOK learning target that specifies the DOK skill students must perform? How could we chunk a standard's learning intention into DOK learning targets and success criteria that are easy to understand and evaluate? How could we organize the DOK learning targets and success criteria into a comprehensive plan that can be used to deliver instruction, respond to intervention, extend learning, and make modifications?

To answer these questions, this chapter provides detail on how to develop a DOK teaching and learning plan. You will learn how to construct a DOK learning target, choose and compose DOK learning goal targets, craft DOK foundational targets, and create DOK extended targets. You will also learn how to confirm the DOK success criteria that specify the DOK response to activities and assessments that address a DOK learning target. The chapter concludes with two reproducible tools to help you begin developing your own DOK teaching and learning plan.

How to Develop a DOK Teaching and Learning Plan

Planning a DOK teaching and learning experience involves the following.

- Constructing DOK learning targets from the standard's learning intention

- Choosing and composing the DOK learning goal target students must achieve or hit to demonstrate grade-level proficiency

- Crafting DOK foundational targets that focus on the baseline knowledge and basic understanding students must acquire and develop

- Creating DOK extended targets that demand students demonstrate their learning beyond the goals and expectations of the standard's learning goal target

- Confirming the DOK success criteria for curricular activities and assessment items that address a DOK learning target

Figure 7.1 is a template that serves as a DOK teaching and learning plan. It reconstructs a standard's learning intention into a learning target statement that includes the DOK skill students must perform. It identifies the DOK response students must provide for activities and assessments that address the standard's learning target. It also organizes the DOK learning targets and success criteria into a comprehensive plan that can be used to deliver instruction, respond to intervention, extend learning, and make modifications.

Construct the DOK Learning Target

After you have deconstructed the standard and designated its DOK level, reconstruct its learning intention into a DOK learning target that features the DOK skill students must perform. Figure 7.2 (page 120) shows how to reconstruct the learning intention for simplifying numerical expressions using the DOK learning target chart from the DOK teaching and learning plan. The chart is ordered in the sentence frame of a learning target. The first column identifies who can or will be demonstrating the learning. Connie Moss and Susan Brookhart (2012) recommend beginning a learning target with a first-person subjective pronoun such as *I* or *we* to "communicate to students that they are the ones who will be doing the learning" (p. 32). The second column states the DOK skill students must perform. The third through fifth columns reconstruct the parts of the learning intention into its objective statement. The final two columns identify the DOK level and the DOK response students must provide to activities and assessments that address the learning intention.

RECONSTRUCTING DOK LEARNING TARGETS						
Who can or will?	What is the DOK skill?	What is the cognitive action?	What is the instructional focus?	What is the instructional purpose?	What is the DOK level?	What is the DOK response?
I can	Specific mental processing	To + verb	Noun or noun phrase	Scope and stipulations	DOK 1 DOK 2 DOK 3 DOK 4	Extent of the response

DELIVERING INSTRUCTION

DOK Foundational Target	DOK Learning Goal Target	DOK Extended Target
I can . . . • Craft DOK learning targets that focus on the vocabulary knowledge students must understand (DOK level) • Craft DOK learning targets that focus on the declarative knowledge students must acquire (DOK level) • Craft DOK learning targets that focus on the procedural knowledge students must develop (DOK level)	I can . . . • Compose a DOK learning target from the standard's learning intention (DOK level) • Catalogue each DOK learning target separately (DOK level)	I can . . . • Create DOK learning targets that demand students demonstrate their learning beyond the standard's learning goal target (DOK Level)

DOK Success Criteria
Students must . . . • Decide the range of DOK responses activities and assessments could demand students to provide and chunk them into DOK success criteria

Figure 7.1: DOK teaching and learning plan.

WHO CAN OR WILL?	WHAT IS THE DOK SKILL?	WHAT IS THE COGNITIVE ACTION?	WHAT IS THE FOCUS?	WHAT IS THE PURPOSE?	WHAT IS THE DOK LEVEL?	WHAT IS THE DOK RESPONSE?
I can	Apply knowledge, concepts, and skills	To simplify	Numerical expressions	• That do not involve exponents • Including up to two levels of grouping	DOK 2 (moderate)	Establish and explain with examples

Figure 7.2: Reconstructed DOK learning target featuring the DOK skill students must perform.

A DOK learning target breaks down—or chunks—a standard's learning intention into simple statements that are clear and concise. Including the DOK skill makes the goals and expectations explicit and easy to understand. Figure 7.3 shows how to chunk the objectives of the English language arts standard into individual DOK learning targets. Notice how the DOK skill specifies the mental processing students must perform to achieve or hit these targets.

WHO CAN OR WILL?	WHAT IS THE DOK SKILL?	WHAT IS THE COGNITIVE ACTION?	WHAT IS THE INSTRUCTIONAL FOCUS?	WHAT IS THE INSTRUCTIONAL PURPOSE?	WHAT IS THE DOK LEVEL?	WHAT IS THE DOK RESPONSE?
I can	Apply knowledge, concepts, and skills	To determine	Meaning	As they are used in a text, including the following: • Figurative meaning • Connotative meanings • Technical meaning	DOK 2 (moderate)	Establish and explain with examples
I can	Use complex reasoning supported by evidence	To analyze	Word choice	Specific impact on the following: • Meaning • Tone	DOK 3 (high)	Establish and explain with evidence

Figure 7.3: DOK learning targets chunking the objectives of a learning intention.

Each objective in a standard's learning intention can set the instructional focus and purpose for individual activities and assessments. Consider the DOK learning targets reconstructed from the history standard on the U.S. Civil War and slavery in figure 7.4. Activities and assessments could demand students achieve or hit one or both targets.

WHO CAN OR WILL?	WHAT IS THE DOK SKILL?	WHAT IS THE COGNITIVE ACTION?	WHAT IS THE INSTRUCTIONAL FOCUS?	WHAT IS THE INSTRUCTIONAL PURPOSE?	WHAT IS THE DOK LEVEL?	WHAT IS THE DOK RESPONSE?
I can	Use information and basic reasoning	To explain	The U.S. Civil War	The causes	DOK 2 (moderate)	Establish and explain with examples
I can	Use complex reasoning supported by evidence	To evaluate	Slavery	Its importance as a principal cause of the conflict	DOK 3 (high)	Establish and explain with evidence

Figure 7.4: DOK learning targets setting the instructional focus and purpose.

DOK learning targets also specify the mental processing students must perform with each step in a multistep procedure or process. Figure 7.5 shows how to reconstruct the specific steps from the world language standard into DOK learning targets. Notice how each step specifies students must apply knowledge, concepts, and skills when they identify and explain the similarities and differences in the basic word order of language systems.

WHO CAN OR WILL?	WHAT IS THE DOK SKILL?	WHAT IS THE COGNITIVE ACTION?	WHAT IS THE INSTRUCTIONAL FOCUS?	WHAT IS THE INSTRUCTIONAL PURPOSE?	WHAT IS THE DOK LEVEL?	WHAT IS THE DOK RESPONSE?
I can	Apply knowledge, concepts, and skills	To identify	Basic word order	Similarities and differences in language systems	DOK 2 (moderate)	Establish and explain with examples
I can	Use complex reasoning supported by evidence	To explain	Basic word order	Similarities and differences in language systems	DOK 2 (moderate)	Establish and explain with examples

Figure 7.5: DOK learning targets for a multistep procedure or process.

Choose and Compose DOK Learning Goal Targets

The DOK learning target reconstructed from the standard's learning intention establishes the DOK learning goal target students must achieve or hit to demonstrate grade-level proficiency or perform successfully. According to Carla Moore, Libby Garst, and Robert Marzano (2015), learning goal targets are "derived directly from state or national academic standards and identify what students should know and be able to do by the end of a grade or course" (p. 11). The target is the same DOK level as the standard's learning intention.

To compose the DOK learning goal target, simply rewrite the standard's learning intention into an *I can* or *we will* statement that includes the DOK skill students must perform. You could also reprint the word parts as they are placed and printed in the DOK learning target table. Figure 7.6 shows how to compose the DOK learning goal target for the English language arts standard on text structure's impact on the author's purpose (TEKS.ELA.4.10.B). Be sure to designate the DOK level in parentheses.

DOK LEARNING GOAL TARGET
I can use complex reasoning supported by evidence to explain how the use of text structure contributes to the author's purpose. (DOK 3)

Figure 7.6: How to compose the DOK learning goal target.

If the standard's learning intention features multiple DOK learning targets, chunk and catalogue each objective separately. Be sure to include the DOK skill students must perform and the DOK level in parentheses. Figure 7.7 shows how to compose the DOK learning goal targets for the history standard on the U.S. Civil War and slavery. Each DOK learning goal target can set the instructional focus and purpose for an individual activity or assessment that addresses this standard. However, students must achieve or hit both targets to demonstrate proficiency.

If the DOK learning goal target demands students perform a multistep procedure or process, each step should be numbered in the order it takes place. Figure 7.8 shows how to chunk and count the steps students must complete to achieve the DOK learning goal target reconstructed from the world language standard on basic word order.

DOK LEARNING GOAL TARGET

I can do the following.

- Use information and basic reasoning to explain the causes of the U.S. Civil War (DOK 2)
- Use complex reasoning supported by evidence to evaluate the importance of slavery as a principal cause of the conflict (DOK 3)

Figure 7.7: How to chunk and catalogue DOK learning goal targets separately.

DOK LEARNING GOAL TARGET

I can do the following.

- Apply knowledge, concepts, and skills to identify the similarities and differences in the basic word order of language systems (DOK 2)
- Apply knowledge, concepts, and skills to explain the similarities and differences in the basic word order of language systems (DOK 2)

Figure 7.8: DOK learning goal targets for a multistep procedure or process.

The DOK learning goal target should be as particular and precise as possible. One way to do this is to narrow the instructional purpose to compose two explicit DOK learning targets. Look at the DOK learning goal targets in figure 7.9. Notice how they narrow the instructional purpose to specify the stipulations for what exactly and how deeply students must apply knowledge, concepts, and skills to simplify numerical expressions. Each of these DOK learning goal targets can be addressed by an individual activity or assessment item.

DOK LEARNING GOAL TARGET

I can do the following.

- Apply knowledge, concepts, and skills to simplify numerical expressions that do not involve exponents (DOK 2)
- Apply knowledge, concepts, and skills to simplify numerical expressions that include up to two levels of grouping (DOK 3)

Figure 7.9: How to narrow the instructional purpose of DOK learning targets.

Another way to make a DOK learning goal target more particular and precise is to address and assess the specific stipulations of a standard's learning intention as the instructional focus. For example, the instructional purpose of the learning intention of the English language arts standard specifies three different types of meaning students must apply knowledge, concepts, and skills to determine. Those types of meaning can set the instructional focus for individual DOK learning goal targets. Figure 7.10 shows how to compose DOK learning goal targets that focus on a specific type of meaning students must determine. It also shows how to narrow the instructional purpose of the second objective on analyzing word choice into two discrete DOK learning targets. Each of these can set the instructional focus and purpose of individual activities and assessment items.

DOK LEARNING GOAL TARGET

I can do the following.

- Apply knowledge, concepts, and skills to determine the meaning of words and phrases as they are used in a text (DOK 2)

- Apply knowledge, concepts, and skills to determine the figurative meaning of words and phrases as they are used in a text (DOK 2)

- Apply knowledge, concepts, and skills to determine the connotative meaning of words and phrases as they are used in a text (DOK 2)

- Apply knowledge, concepts, and skills to determine the technical meaning of words and phrases as they are used in a text (DOK 2)

- Use complex reasoning supported by evidence to analyze the impact of a specific word choice on meaning (DOK 2)

- Use complex reasoning supported by evidence to analyze the impact of a specific word choice on tone (DOK 2)

Figure 7.10: How to narrow a DOK learning target by addressing the stipulations of the instructional focus.

The DOK learning goal targets should be explicit in their goals and expectations. They should also be easy to read. Chunking the learning intention and its objectives into individual and itemized DOK learning targets will make the goals and expectations easy to comprehend and communicate.

Craft DOK Foundational Targets

Once the DOK learning goal target is established, the standard's learning intention needs to be deconstructed and chunked further to craft DOK foundational targets that focus on the following.

- The vocabulary knowledge students must understand (for example, words and terms)

- The declarative knowledge students must acquire (for example, facts and concepts)

- The imperative knowledge students must develop (for example, procedures and strategies)

Foundational learning targets address and assess "the prerequisites that students need to master to ultimately achieve the learning goal targets" (Moore et al., 2015, pp. 11–12). The goal and expectation of these targets are for students to acquire and develop the foundational knowledge and functional understanding they need to achieve or hit the learning goal target successfully.

To craft DOK foundational targets, unwrap or unpack the standards to identify the nouns that name the key concepts or content students must learn and the verbs that specify the skills they must develop. Write a DOK learning target statement that features the DOK skill students must perform and a simple definition, description, or explanation of the concept or skill. Figure 7.11 shows how to craft DOK foundational targets for developing and using a model on cells. These DOK foundational targets focus on the subject-specific terms students must know, the disciplinary core ideas students must understand, and the scientific and engineering practices students must learn to use.

DOK FOUNDATIONAL TARGETS

I can do the following.

- Recall information to describe a cell is the smallest structural, functional, and biological unit of all living organisms (DOK 1)

- Recall information to explain the function of a cell as a whole (DOK 1)

- Recall information to describe the parts of a cell (DOK 1)

- Apply knowledge, concepts, and skills to describe the ways the parts of cells contribute to the function (DOK 2)

- Apply knowledge, concepts, and skills to develop a scientific model to describe unobservable mechanisms (DOK 2)

- Apply knowledge, concepts, and skills to use a scientific model to describe a phenomenon (DOK 2)

Figure 7.11: How to craft DOK foundational targets.

DOK foundational targets could address "prerequisite knowledge and processes not always explicitly stated in the academic standard" (Moore et al., 2015, p. 18). This knowledge comes from the curriculum or supporting grade-level standards. For example, figure 7.12 (page 126) features DOK foundational targets that focus

DOK FOUNDATIONAL TARGETS

I can do the following.

- Recall information to describe a numerical expression as a combination of numbers and mathematical operation symbols (e.g., +, -, x, ÷) (DOK 1)

- Recall information to describe exponents that state how many times a number is multiplied by itself (DOK 1)

- Recall information to explain that simplifying is a mathematical process that requires putting an equation in its simplest form to make it easier to use and solve (DOK 1)

- Recall information to explain that grouping involves dividing items or things into equal groups (DOK 1)

- Recall information to describe prime numbers are whole numbers that can be divided only by 1 and the number itself (DOK 1)

- Recall information to describe composite numbers are whole numbers that can be divided by two or more numbers or factors (DOK 1)

- Recall information to describe the meaning of parentheses and brackets in a numerical expression (DOK 1)

- Apply knowledge, concepts, and skills to identify prime and composite numbers (DOK 2)

- Apply knowledge, concepts, and skills to understand how parentheses and brackets are used in a numerical expression (DOK 2)

Figure 7.12: DOK foundational targets addressing prerequisite knowledge or processes not specified in the standard.

on vocabulary, declarative, and procedural knowledge not addressed in the mathematics standard's learning intention or goal target. However, students must understand these terms, details, and procedures and use them correctly when they simplify numerical expressions.

The level of Depth of Knowledge demanded by DOK foundational targets depends on the instructional focus of the targets. DOK foundational targets focusing on vocabulary or declarative knowledge will usually be a DOK 1 because they require students to recall information to describe or explain. The level of Depth of Knowledge demanded by DOK foundational targets that focus on procedural knowledge will determine the depth and extent to which students must understand and use a procedure or strategy to hit the DOK learning goal target. However, the level of Depth of Knowledge demanded by DOK foundational targets will not exceed the level demanded by the DOK learning goal target reconstructed from the standard's learning intention. They could be comparable, but not deeper or more demanding.

Create DOK Extended Targets

DOK extended targets demand that students demonstrate their learning beyond the goals and expectations of a standard's learning intention or goal targets. The purpose of these extended learning targets is to prompt and encourage students "to think about the same content in more complex ways" (Moore et al., 2015, p. 12). For example, the DOK extended target in figure 7.13 stretches the scope and stipulations of the English language standard by encouraging students to use extended reasoning supported by expertise to analyze the impact of specific word choice in two or more texts that address the same subject but are by different authors. This deepens the level of Depth of Knowledge students must demonstrate to a DOK 4.

DOK LEARNING GOAL TARGET
I can think extensively to analyze the impact of a specific word choice on the meaning and tone of two or more texts that address the same topic but are in different genres or by different authors. (DOK 4)

Figure 7.13: DOK extended target.

DOK extended targets could be cognitively complex targets that demand students demonstrate "a level of processing or cognitive complexity that compels students to delve more deeply into the content of the academic standard" (Moore et al., 2015, p. 21). One way to deepen cognitive demand is to change the context or intensify the instructional purpose of the DOK learning goal target. Consider the DOK learning targets in figure 7.14 (page 128). They all have the same performance expectation. However, the scope and stipulations of the DOK extended targets expand the depth and degree to which students must simplify numerical expressions. This deepens both the DOK skill students must perform and the level of Depth of Knowledge students must demonstrate beyond the standard's learning intention or goal target.

The DOK extended targets do not have to demand students demonstrate their learning at a level of Depth of Knowledge deeper than the standard's learning intention or goal target. In fact, the DOK level of a goal and extended target could be comparable. For example, the DOK learning goal and extended targets for the world language standard in figure 7.15 (page 128) are all a DOK 2 because they challenge students to apply knowledge, concepts, and skills. They just differ in their instructional focus.

DOK LEARNING GOAL TARGET	DOK EXTENDED TARGETS
I can do the following. • Apply knowledge, concepts, and skills to simplify numerical expressions that do not involve exponents (DOK 2) • Apply knowledge, concepts, and skills to simplify numerical expressions up to two levels of grouping (DOK 2)	I can do the following. • Think strategically to simplify numerical expressions with exponents in nonroutine problems (DOK 3) • Think strategically to simplify numerical expressions in nonroutine problems that include multiple levels of grouping (DOK 3) • Think strategically to simplify numerical expressions in nonroutine problems with multiple variables (DOK 3) • Think strategically to simplify numerical expressions in nonroutine problems that involve several mathematical operations (DOK 3)

Figure 7.14: DOK extended targets that deepen the cognitive demand.

DOK LEARNING GOAL TARGET	DOK EXTENDED TARGETS
I can do the following. • Apply knowledge, concepts, and skills to identify the similarities and differences in the basic word order of language systems (DOK 2) • Apply knowledge, concepts, and skills to explain the similarities and differences in the basic word order of language systems (DOK 2)	I can do the following. • Apply knowledge, concepts, and skills to identify the similarities and differences in the formal and informal forms of language systems (DOK 2) • Apply knowledge, concepts, and skills to explain the similarities and differences in the formal and informal forms of language systems (DOK 2)

Figure 7.15: DOK extended targets at the same DOK level as the learning goal targets.

DOK extended targets can also extend the teaching and learning experience across the curriculum. For example, in figure 7.16, the DOK extended targets for the history standard on the U.S. Civil War and slavery are reconstructed from English language arts standards that encourage students to think extensively how they could conduct short research projects. These are DOK extended targets not only because of their DOK levels but also because they demand that students connect, transfer, and utilize what they are learning in multiple content areas. Be sure to chunk the standards into clear and concise DOK extended targets if the learning intentions are lengthy and wordy.

DOK LEARNING GOAL TARGET	DOK EXTENDED TARGETS
I can do the following. • Use information and basic reasoning to explain the causes of the U.S. Civil War (DOK 2) • Use complex reasoning supported by evidence to evaluate the importance of slavery as a principal cause of the conflict (DOK 3)	I can do the following. • Think extensively to conduct short research projects to answer a question (including a self-generated question), drawing on several sources and generating additional related, focused questions that allow for multiple avenues of exploration (DOK 4)

Figure 7.16: DOK extended targets extended across the curriculum.

The simplest way to create DOK extended targets is to encourage students to think extensively or use extended reasoning supported by expertise to address, explain, or respond to a real-world scenario or situation. In fact, extending a standard's learning intention could be as simple as adding that stipulation to the instructional purpose. Figure 7.17 shows how adding the stipulation "address, explain, or respond to a real-world scenario or situation" extends the standard on cells to a DOK 4. Having students choose the real-world scenario or situation to address, explain, or respond to will make the DOK teaching and learning experience even more extensive.

DOK LEARNING GOAL TARGET	DOK EXTENDED TARGET
I can think strategically how to develop and use a scientific model to describe the following. • The function of a cell (DOK 3) • Ways the parts of cells contribute to the function (DOK 3)	I can think extensively how to develop and use a model to address, explain, or respond to a real-world scenario or situation that involves the following. • The function of cells (DOK 4) • Ways the parts of cells contribute to the function (DOK 3)

Figure 7.17: DOK extended targets with added stipulation.

Adding certain conditions or criteria to the context of a subject-specific standard will extend the DOK learning target to a DOK 4. Table 7.1 (page 130) lists conditions and criteria that will extend the instructional purpose of DOK learning targets in certain content areas to a DOK 4. These conditions and criteria also could be used to create DOK 4 extended targets for academic standards, activities, and assessments that address specific kinds of knowledge. For example, DOK extended targets that focus on factual knowledge encourage students to use extended reasoning supported by expertise to explore and explain *two or more texts or works*. DOK extended targets focusing on procedural knowledge encourage students to understand and use what they have learned in *a real-world scenario or situation*.

TABLE 7.1: Conditions and Criteria for DOK 4 Extended Targets

Content Area	Contexts for DOK 4 Extended Targets
Mathematics	". . . address, explain, or respond to a real-world scenario or situation . . ."
Literature and Language Arts	". . . two or more texts that address the same topic . . ." ". . . two or more texts written by the same or different authors . . ." ". . . two or more texts written in the same, different, or across genres . . ."
Science	". . . address, explain, or respond to a real-world scenario or situation . . . "
History	" . . . two or more texts that address the same topic . . ." ". . . two or more texts written by the same or different authors . . ." ". . . two or more texts written in the same or different time periods. . ." " . . .two or more incidents, individuals, or issues . . ." ". . .impact on history, the present, and the future . . ." ". . .impact on society historically, presently, and in the future . . ."
Civics	". . . address, explain, or respond to a real-world scenario or situation . . ." " . . . two or more texts that address the same topic . . ." ". . . two or more texts written by the same or different authors . . ." ". . . two or more texts written in the same or different time periods. . ." ". . . two or more ideas or issues . . ." ". . . impact on different areas and aspects of society. . ." ". . . influence on different areas and aspects of society. . ."
Geography	". . . address, explain, or respond to a real-world scenario or situation . . ."
Economics	". . . address, explain, or respond to a real-world scenario or situation . . ."

Visual and Fine Arts	" . . . two or more pieces or performances that address the same topic . . ." ". . . two or more pieces or performances produced by the same or different artists or musicians . . ." ". . . two or more pieces or performances produced in the same genre, different genres, or across genres . . ."
World Language	". . . in real-world scenario or situation . . ."
Health and Physical Education	". . . in a real-world scenario or situation . . ."
Career and Technical Education	". . . address, explain, or respond to a real-world scenario or situation . . ."

Confirm the Range of DOK Success Criteria

The DOK learning targets should also be rephrased into DOK success criteria statements that describe "what it means to do quality work" (Moss & Brookhart, 2012, p. 47). Figure 7.18 shows the DOK success criteria that address the world language standard's learning intention and goal target.

DOK LEARNING GOAL TARGET	DOK SUCCESS CRITERIA
I can do the following. • Apply knowledge, concepts, and skills to identify the similarities and differences in the basic word order of language systems (DOK 2) • Apply knowledge, concepts, and skills to explain the similarities and differences in the basic word order of language systems (DOK 2)	Students must establish and explain with examples what the similarities and differences are between the basic word order of language systems (DOK 2)

Figure 7.18: DOK success criteria.

The DOK success criteria describe how the range of DOK levels at which activities and assessments addressing a specific standard could demand students to respond. Consider the DOK success criteria in figure 7.19 (page 132) for the mathematics standard on simplifying numerical expressions. Notice how the DOK responses students might offer range from answering correctly (DOK 1) to examining and exploring with examples and evidence (DOK 4). They also address all the DOK learning targets chunked, crafted, and created from the standard's learning intention.

DOK SUCCESS CRITERIA
Students must do the following.

- Answer correctly what a numerical expression is (DOK 1)
- Answer correctly what exponents do (DOK 1)
- Answer correctly what simplifying involves (DOK 1)
- Answer correctly what grouping involves (DOK 1)
- Establish and explain with examples how numerical expressions that do not involve exponents can be simplified (DOK 2)✔*
- Establish and explain with examples how numerical expressions that include up to two levels of grouping can be simplified (DOK 2)✔*
- Examine and explain with evidence how numerical expressions with exponents could be simplified (DOK 3)+
- Examine and explain with evidence how numerical expressions with exponents could be simplified (DOK 3)+
- Examine and explain with evidence how numerical expressions with several operations could be simplified (DOK 3)+
- Examine and explain with evidence how numerical expressions with different mathematical operations could be simplified (DOK 3)+
- Examine and explain with evidence how numerical expressions that include multiple levels of grouping could be simplified (DOK 3)+
- Examine and explain with evidence how numerical expressions with multiple variables could be simplified (DOK 3)+
- Examine and explain with evidence how numerical expressions that reflect or represent a real-world scenario or situation could be simplified (DOK 3)+
- Explore and explain with examples and evidence how to address, explain, or respond to a real-world scenario or situation that involves simplifying numerical expressions (DOK 4)+

Figure 7.19: DOK success criteria for all DOK levels.

Notice some of these DOK success criteria are also tagged with a symbol. These symbols identify assessment ceilings and inform degrees of alignment. For example, the DOK success criteria with a check mark (✔) are rephrased from the standard's learning intention or goal target. The activities and assessment items they address are fully aligned to the standard. The ones marked with an asterisk (*) identify the DOK success criteria ceiling—the deepest level at which test items could demand students respond. The ones with a plus sign (+) address the DOK extended targets and demand students to demonstrate their learning beyond the standard's learning intention and goal target. Tagging the DOK success criteria with these symbols helps with planning the pathway to proficiency and the progression of performance.

The DOK success criteria can also serve as a rubric or scoring guide that shows students how their work will be evaluated and what is expected from them. For example, the DOK success criteria in figure 7.20 show how the scientific model on cells will be evaluated. They also stipulate what the model must feature or include. Educators can use the DOK success criteria to validate if the performance or product is acceptable and complete. Students can use the DOK success criteria to verify whether their performance or product addresses all the requirements.

DOK SUCCESS CRITERIA

Students must do the following.

- Answer correctly what a cell is (DOK 1)
- Answer correctly what the function of a cell is as a whole (DOK 1)✓
- Establish and explain with examples the ways the parts of cells contribute to the function (DOK 2)✓
- Establish and explain with examples how a scientific model can be developed to describe unobservable mechanisms (DOK 2)✓
- Examine and explain with evidence how a scientific model could be developed and used to describe phenomena (DOK 3)✓*

Figure 7.20: DOK success criteria as a rubric.

The DOK success criteria replace the cognitive action verb within the learning intention or target with a question stem that prompts students to comprehend and communicate what they are learning. These question stems will introduce the good questions that will address and assess student learning. (We'll learn more about how to pose good DOK questions in chapter 8, page 141.) Consider the DOK success criteria in figure 7.21 (page 134). Notice how the DOK success criteria replace the cognitive action verb *to analyze* with a good question stem that asks, "What impact?" This figure also shows how the DOK success criteria can be transformed into good questions that address and assess the DOK learning target.

DOK LEARNING TARGET	DOK SUCCESS CRITERIA	GOOD DOK QUESTION
I can do the following. • Use complex reasoning supported by evidence to analyze the impact of a specific word choice on meaning (DOK 3) • Use complex reasoning supported by evidence to analyze the impact of a specific word choice on tone (DOK 3)	Students must do the following. • Examine and explain with evidence what impact a specific word choice has on meaning (DOK 3) • Examine and explain with evidence what impact a specific word choice has on tone (DOK 3)	• What impact does a specific word choice have on the meaning of the word and the text as a whole? (DOK 3) • What impact does a specific word choice have on the tone of the word and the text as a whole? (DOK 3)

Figure 7.21: DOK success criteria translated into good DOK questions.

Summary

The learning intention of academic standards, activities, and assessments can be difficult to comprehend and communicate. Reconstructing and chunking them into learning targets and success criteria will make them easier to read and understand. Including the DOK skill students will perform and the DOK response students must provide will make them more explicit and easier to evaluate. When reconstructing learning intentions into DOK learning targets and success criteria, keep the following in mind.

• DOK learning targets start with *I can* or *we will* so students will personalize each target's goals and expectations. DOK success criteria start with *students must* to establish the principles of performance for all students.

• The DOK learning goal target establishes the goals and expectations for demonstrating proficiency. Each individual objective within a standard's learning intention is a DOK learning goal target students must achieve or hit to perform successfully in a specific subject at a given grade level.

• The DOK foundational targets address the background knowledge and basic understanding students need to achieve or hit the DOK learning goal targets successfully. This includes the vocabulary students must understand, the declarative knowledge students must acquire, and the imperative knowledge students must develop.

- The DOK extended targets demand that students demonstrate their learning beyond the goals and expectations of the standard. Their DOK levels do not have to be deeper; however, the instructional focus or purpose should differ from the DOK learning goal target.

- The DOK success criteria establish the principles for performance. They inform what the academic standard, activity, or assessment expects from all students and how student learning will be evaluated.

The DOK learning targets and success criteria featured in this chapter are reconstructs from grade-level standards. However, any learning intention—be it an IEP goal, a language expectation, or a curricular objective—could be reconstructed into a DOK learning target or success criteria. Determine the DOK skill, decide the DOK response, and reconstruct the learning intention into a learning target or success criteria statement that features these DOK descriptors. Watch how they make the IEP, language, or curricular learning intention explicit, easy to read, and easy to evaluate.

Using Depth of Knowledge

Either on your own or as part of a teacher team, complete the following tasks.

Use the learning intention you deconstructed in chapters 5 and 6 or choose another one. Create a DOK teaching and learning plan with DOK learning targets and success criteria that specify the DOK skills students must perform and the DOK response students must provide. Use the reproducible "DOK Learning Target Grid" (page 138) to do the following.

1. Decide who can or will be doing the learning. Use *I can* or *we will* to introduce the DOK learning target. Use *students must* to introduce the DOK success criteria.

2. List the DOK skill that specifies the mental processing students must perform. This will be featured in your DOK learning target.

3. Reconstruct the learning intention of the standard by placing its parts under the appropriate columns. Now you have your DOK learning goal target statement.

4. Record the DOK level. This will be stated in parentheses after the DOK learning target in the DOK teaching and learning plan.

5. Decide the DOK response students must provide. This will be stated in the DOK success criteria for this learning target. It should be aligned to the DOK skill students must perform.

6. Place an asterisk next to the most cognitively demanding DOK response. That's the DOK success criteria ceiling.

7. Unpack or unwrap the standard to identify the nouns and verbs that name the following.

    a. The words and terms students must know. This is the vocabulary knowledge students must understand.

    b. The details, facts, and information students must understand. This is the declarative knowledge students must acquire.

    c. The procedures and strategies students must use. This is the imperative knowledge students must develop.

8. Craft DOK learning targets that briefly describe or explain these words, terms, facts, concepts, procedures, and strategies. These will identify the instructional focus of the DOK foundational targets.

9. Extend the instructional focus and purpose beyond the standard's learning intention by changing the content knowledge students will learn or the context in which students must demonstrate their learning. This will create the DOK extended targets.

10. Piece together the word parts from the first six columns into a DOK learning target. Share the DOK learning target with the students. Chunk the instructional focus or multiple objectives if necessary.

Use the reproducible "DOK Teaching and Learning Plan Template" (page 139) to do the following.

1. Compose the reconstructed learning intention as a DOK learning target statement that begins with *I can* or *we will*. That's the DOK learning goal target for demonstrating proficiency.

2. Chunk and catalogue all the objectives reconstructed into DOK learning targets under the column marked DOK Learning Goal Target. Students will need to achieve or hit all these learning targets to demonstrate grade-level proficiency.

3. Craft DOK foundational targets that focus on the nouns and verbs unpacked from the standard's learning intention. Provide a brief description or explanation of the term, fact, concept, or procedure. This

will be the prerequisite knowledge students must understand, acquire, and develop.

4. Create DOK extended targets that demand students demonstrate their learning beyond the standard's learning intention. These could be the following.

    a. Cognitively complex targets that demand students demonstrate their learning at a DOK level that's comparable to or deeper than the standard's DOK level

    b. Learning targets that differ from the standard's instructional purpose or address a different topic within the same content area

    c. DOK learning targets reconstructed from a standard from a different grade level or content area

    d. DOK 4 learning targets that encourage students to use extensive reasoning supported by expertise to analyze two or more texts or topics or think extensively to address, explain, or respond to a real-world scenario or situation

5. Decide the DOK response students must provide and rephrase the DOK learning target into a DOK success criteria statement that begins with *students must*. List the range of DOK levels at which activities and assessments could demand students respond.

6. Identify specific DOK success criteria with the following.

    a. A check mark (✔) next to the DOK success criteria that address the standard's DOK learning goal target. These are aligned to the standard.

    b. An asterisk (*) next to the most cognitively demanding DOK success criteria that address the standard's DOK learning goal target. This is the DOK ceiling of assessment.

    c. A plus sign (+) next to the DOK success criteria that demand students to demonstrate their learning beyond the standard. These will not be assessed on standardized summative or interim assessments.

DOK Learning Target Grid

WHO CAN OR WILL?	WHAT IS THE DOK SKILL?	WHAT IS THE COGNITIVE ACTION?	WHAT IS THE INSTRUCTIONAL FOCUS?	WHAT IS THE INSTRUCTIONAL PURPOSE?	WHAT IS THE DOK LEVEL?	WHAT IS THE DOK RESPONSE?

*Deconstructing Depth of **Knowledge**: A Method and Model for Deeper Teaching and Learning*
© 2022 Solution Tree Press • SolutionTree.com • Visit **go.SolutionTree.com/instruction**
to download this free reproducible.

DOK Teaching and Learning Plan Template

DOK FOUNDATIONAL TARGET	DOK LEARNING GOAL TARGET	DOK EXTENDED TARGET
I can do the following:	I can do the following:	I can do the following:

DOK SUCCESS CRITERIA
Students must do the following:

CHAPTER EIGHT

How to Ask and Address Good Questions for Depth of Knowledge

In chapter 7 (page 117), we learned how to reconstruct the learning intention of academic standards into DOK learning targets and DOK success criteria. However, what designates the level of Depth of Knowledge demanded by a good question? Why does determining the DOK level of questions involve looking beyond the question stem? How could good questions be used to develop and deliver DOK teaching and learning experiences that promote inquiry? How might we, as educators, and our students, pose good questions that prompt deeper reflection and responses?

To answer these questions, this chapter presents essential information on how to understand and use good questions to foster and promote Depth of Knowledge. You will learn how to determine the DOK level of a good question based on the DOK response students must provide. You will create good questions that differ in their DOK levels. You will learn how to use good questions to deliver DOK teaching and learning experiences that are inquiry-based. You will also learn how to encourage students to ask good DOK questions. The chapter concludes with tasks to help you craft good questions for the DOK teaching and learning plan you developed in chapter 7 (page 139).

How to Understand and Use Good Questions for Depth of Knowledge

DOK teaching and learning experiences that are inquiry-based prompt students to reflect upon and respond to the following overarching questions that address the core ideas and enduring understandings of each DOK level.

- What is the knowledge?

- How and why can the knowledge be understood and used?

- How and why could the knowledge be understood and used?

- What else could be done with the knowledge?

Figure 8.1 represents the DOK blocks as an inquiry-based learning method and model that address these good overarching questions. Each of the DOK blocks also features examples of specific good question stems that will prompt students to perform a specific mental process at a designated DOK level. However, as with the verbs of learning intentions, it's the words and phrases that follow the question stem that determine the level of Depth of Knowledge at which students must reflect and respond.

The following sections will discuss four essential steps to help you understand and use good questions for Depth of Knowledge.

- Determine the DOK level of a good question.

- Create good questions for Depth of Knowledge.

- Deliver an inquiry-based DOK teaching and learning experience using good questions.

- Encourage students to ask good questions for Depth of Knowledge.

Determine the DOK Level of a Good Question

The cognitive rigor of a good question depends on the following (Francis, 2016a).

- The type of thinking and kind of knowledge students must demonstrate as categorized by Bloom's revised taxonomy

- The depth and extent at which students must understand and use their knowledge and thinking—or learning—according to the DOK levels

Good questions start with one of the six Ws (*who, what, where, when, why, which*) and one H (*how*). Like cognitive action verbs, question stems prompt the type and level of thinking students must demonstrate. The words and phrases that follow the

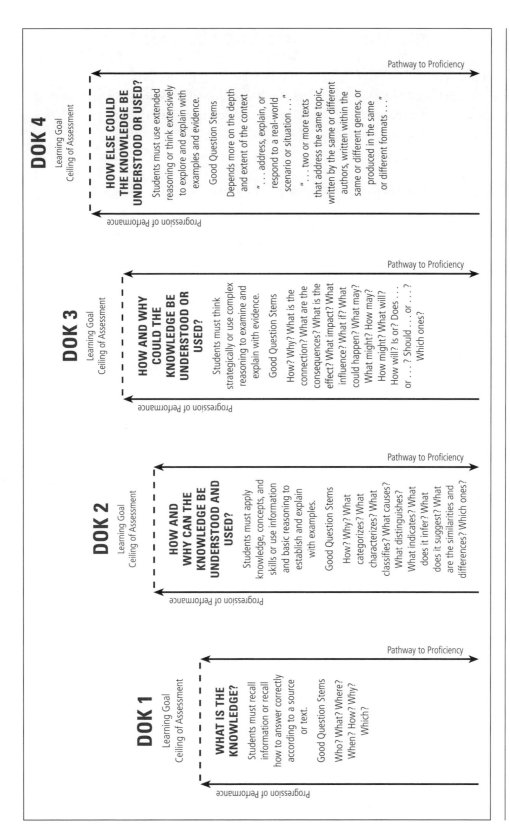

Figure 8.1: DOK blocks featuring good question stems for Depth of Knowledge.

question stem determine the demand of the DOK skill students must perform and DOK response students must provide. Consider the good questions in figure 8.2. Each of them asks to reflect *how*. However, it's the words and phrases that follow the question stem that specify what exactly and how deeply students must reflect and respond *how*.

GOOD QUESTIONS FOR DEPTH OF KNOWLEDGE	DOK SKILL	DOK RESPONSE	DOK LEVEL
How do you create a chronological sequence of multiple events?	Recall how to	Answer correctly	DOK 1 (low)
How can you create and use a chronological sequence of related events to compare developments that happened at the same time?	Apply knowledge, concepts, and skills	Establish and explain with examples	DOK 2 (moderate)
How could you create and use a chronological sequence of events to compare developments that happened at the same time?	Think strategically	Examine and explain with evidence	DOK 3 (high)
How could you create and use a chronological sequence of events to evaluate how historical events and developments were shaped by unique circumstances of time and place as well as broader historical contexts?	Think extensively	Explore and explain with examples and evidence	DOK 4 (extensive)

Figure 8.2: How to use basic stems in good DOK questions to designate the DOK level.

The DOK level of a good question also depends on the type of question asked. Table 8.1 is an extended version of the Cognitive Rigor Questioning (CRQ) Framework introduced in my book *Now That's a Good Question!* (Francis, 2016a). The Depth of Knowledge demanded by these good questions depends on the extent of the response they demand students provide. For example, good analytical questions demand students establish and explain with examples (DOK 2), examine and explain with evidence (DOK 3), or explore and explain with examples and evidence (DOK 4). Some good questions, however, will always and only demand that students respond at a

TABLE 8.1: DOK Levels of Cognitive Rigor Questions

Cognitive Rigor Question	Good Question	DOK Level
Factual	Who? What? Where? When? How? Why? Which?	DOK 1
	What are the words and terms students must understand?	
	What are the specific details, facts, or information?	
	What is the concept or procedure?	
	What is the correct answer?	
Analytical	How and why can concepts or procedures be used?	DOK 2
	What characterizes? What classifies?	DOK 3
	What are the similarities and differences?	DOK 4
	What distinguishes or indicates?	
	What is the relationship? (Cause and effect)	
	What does it infer or suggest?	
	What is the pattern or trend?	
Reflective	What is the effect?	DOK 2
	What are the connections?	DOK 3
	What are the consequences?	DOK 4
	What impact or influence?	
	What is the rationale?	
	What are the reasons?	
	What is the outcome, result, or solution?	
Hypothetical	What if? What would happen? What could happen? What may or might? What will? How will?	DOK 3
		DOK 4
	What are the alternatives or options?	
	What is the possibility, potential, or probability?	
Argumentative	Is . . . or . . .? Does . . . or . . .? Should . . . or . . .? Which ones?	DOK 3
	Which option, opinion, or outcome is the best, most effective, or most appropriate?	DOK 4
	How should an issue or situation be addressed, handled, resolved, or settled?	
Affective	What do you believe, think, or feel?	DOK 2
	What is your opinion, perspective, or thoughts?	DOK 3
	How can you? How could you?	DOK 4
	What could you create, design, develop, or do?	
Personal	What questions do you have?	DOK 1
	What do you want to know or understand?	DOK 2
	What do you want to learn?	DOK 3
	How do you want to use what you have learned?	DOK 4

Source: Adapted from Francis, 2016a.

specific DOK level. For example, factual questions are only a DOK 1 because they always require students to answer correctly. Good hypothetical and argumentative questions are DOK 3s and DOK 4s because they demand students examine or explore and explain with evidence.

The simplest way to determine the level of Depth of Knowledge of a good question is to decide the DOK response students must provide. If the good question requires students to answer correctly, it's a DOK 1. If the good question challenges students to establish and explain with examples, it's a DOK 2. A good DOK 3 question will engage students to examine and explain with evidence. A good DOK 4 question will encourage students to explore and explain with examples and evidence over an extended period. However, extended time is a characteristic of a good DOK 4 question, not a criterion.

Create Good Questions for Depth of Knowledge

The simplest way to create a good DOK question is to place the question stems, "How do you?", "How can you?", or "How could you?" in front of a learning intention. This transforms the learning intention from an imperative statement into a good affective question stem that asks students to reflect and respond what they (or you) can personally do with the content knowledge (Francis, 2016a). Figure 8.3 features examples of learning intentions rewritten as good DOK affective questions.

LEARNING INTENTION	GOOD DOK QUESTION
Express measurements in a larger unit in terms of a smaller unit. (DOK 1)	How do you express measurements in a larger unit in terms of a smaller unit? (DOK 1)
Simplify numerical expressions that do not involve exponents, including up to two levels of grouping. (DOK 2)	How can you simplify numerical expressions that do not involve exponents, including up to two levels of grouping? (DOK 2)
Determine the figurative meaning of words and phrases as they are used in a text. (DOK 2)	How can you determine the figurative meaning of words and phrases as they are used in a text? (DOK 2)
Develop and use a model to describe the function of a cell as a whole and ways the parts of cells contribute to the function. (DOK 3)	How could you develop and use a model to describe the function of a cell as a whole and ways the parts of cells contribute to the function? (DOK 3)

Figure 8.3: How to rewrite learning intentions as good DOK questions.

Another simple way to create good DOK questions is to replace the first-person introduction of a DOK learning target (for example, *I can* or *we will*) and instead ask, "How could you . . .?" Figure 8.4 shows how to rephrase a DOK learning target into a good question. It's the teacher's decision whether to include the DOK skill in the good DOK question to make the expectations more explicit and easier to understand or evaluate.

DOK LEARNING TARGET	GOOD AFFECTIVE QUESTION
I can use complex reasoning supported by evidence to explain why addition and subtraction strategies work, using the following. • Place value (DOK 3) • The properties of operations (DOK 3)	How could you explain why addition and subtraction strategies work using the following? • Place value (DOK 3) • The properties of operations (DOK 3)
I can use complex reasoning supported by evidence to explain how variations in genetic characteristics among individuals of the same species may provide advantages in the following. • Surviving (DOK 3) • Finding mates (DOK 3) • Reproducing (DOK 3)	How could you explain how variations in genetic characteristics among individuals of the same species may provide advantages in the following? • Surviving (DOK 3) • Finding mates (DOK 3) • Reproducing (DOK 3)
I can use complex reasoning supported by evidence to analyze how the elements of music relate to the following. • Style (DOK 3) • Mood (DOK 3)	How could you analyze how the elements of music relate to the following? • Style (DOK 3) • Mood (DOK 3)

Figure 8.4: How to rephrase DOK learning targets as good DOK questions.

Many learning intentions feature a question stem (or parts of one) that can be used to create a good DOK question. These question stems usually follow the initial cognitive action verb of the performance expectation. To create the good DOK question, remove the cognitive action verb and rephrase the imperative statement into an interrogative one that ends with a question mark. Figure 8.5 (page 148) shows how to create good DOK questions from learning intentions that feature a question stem or parts of a question stem.

LEARNING INTENTION	GOOD DOK QUESTION
Explain how the use of text structure contributes to the author's purpose. (DOK 3)	How does the use of text structure contribute to the author's purpose? (DOK 3)
Explain how the perspectives of people in the present shape interpretations of the past. (DOK 4)	How could the perspectives of people in the present shape interpretations of the past? (DOK 4)
Explain the differences and similarities between the word structures (derivation, prefixes, suffixes, and so on) in the target language and students' own language. (DOK 2)	What are the differences and similarities between the following word structures in the target language and students' own language? • Derivation (DOK 2) • Prefixes (DOK 2) • Suffixes (DOK 2)
Explain how the method of display, the location, and the experience of a work of art influence how it is perceived and valued. (DOK 3)	What influence could the following have on the perception and value of a work of art? • The method of display (DOK 3) • The location (DOK 3) • The experience (DOK 3)

Figure 8.5: How to create good DOK questions from learning intentions that feature a question stem or parts of a question stem.

DOK success criteria can also be rephrased as good DOK questions. To create the questions, first remove *students must* and the DOK response from the success criteria statement. Then rephrase the success criteria statement as an interrogative sentence that begins with the question stem featured in the DOK success criteria. Figure 8.6 shows how DOK success criteria can be rephrased as good DOK questions.

If the learning intention or target does not feature a question stem, replace the cognitive action verb with a question stem that will prompt students to reflect and respond at the DOK level demanded. Figure 8.7 (page 150) is an updated version of the Bloom's inverted questioning pyramid featured in my book *Now That's a Good Question!* (Francis, 2016a). Notice how Bloom's levels contain question stems instead of cognitive action verbs. This figure also reintroduces *Synthesize* as a cognitive category within the taxonomy. Good questions at this level ask students to consider and convey

DOK SUCCESS CRITERIA	GOOD DOK QUESTION
Students must examine and explain with evidence how proportional relationships could be analyzed and used to solve real-world and mathematical problems. (DOK 3)	How could proportional relationships be analyzed and used to solve real-world and mathematical problems? (DOK 3)
Students will establish and explain with examples what distinguishes the following about public policies in multiple settings. • Their purpose (DOK 2) • Their implementation (DOK 2) • Their consequences (DOK 2)	What distinguishes the following about public policies in multiple settings? • Their purpose (DOK 2) • Their implementation (DOK 2) • Their consequences (DOK 2)
Students must establish and explain with examples how components in visual imagery convey messages. (DOK 2)	How do components of visual images convey messages? (DOK 2)
Students must examine and explain with evidence what impact food choices have on the following. • Physical activity (DOK 3) • Youth sports (DOK 3) • Personal health (DOK 3)	What impact do food choices have on the following? • Physical activity (DOK 3) • Youth sports (DOK 3) • Personal health (DOK 3)

Figure 8.6: How to rephrase DOK success criteria as good DOK questions.

their attitudes, beliefs, and feelings about what they are learning. That's why the level features question stems that emphasize *you*. Changing the cognitive action verb to one of these Bloom's question stems will help decide the DOK response students must provide. However, keep in mind, it's the words and phrases that come after the question stem that designate the DOK level of a good question.

The conceptual or content-specific nouns and cognitive action verbs from unpacked or unwrapped standards can also be used to set the subject of good DOK questions. Look at the good DOK questions created from the mathematics standard in figure 8.8 (page 151). Notice how the conceptual nouns and cognitive action verbs state the subject for good DOK questions that ask students to describe or explain subject-specific terms, concepts, and procedures.

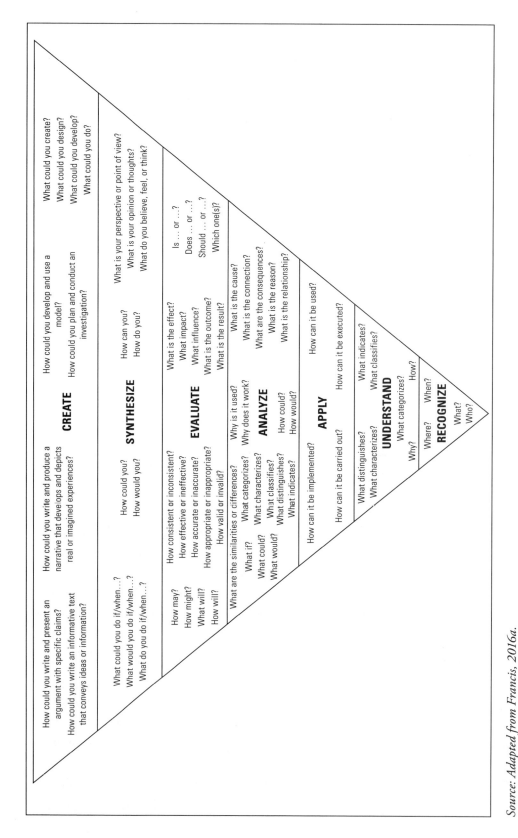

Source: Adapted from Francis, 2016a.

Figure 8.7: Bloom's inverted questioning pyramid.

LEARNING INTENTION	Find whole-number quotients of whole numbers with up to four-digit dividends and two-digit divisors, using strategies based on place value, the properties of operations, or the relationship between multiplication and division. (DOK 2)
What Is the Subject-Specific Terminology? **What Are the Details or Elements?**	**How Can Concepts and Procedures Be Understood and Used?**
• What is a quotient? (DOK 1) • What is a whole number? (DOK 1) • What is a whole-number quotient? (DOK 1) • What is a digit? (DOK 1) • What is a dividend? (DOK 1) • What is a four-digit dividend? (DOK 1) • What is a divisor? (DOK 1) • What is a two-digit divisor? (DOK 1) • What is place value? (DOK 1) • What are the properties of operations? (DOK 1) • What is multiplication? (DOK 1) • What is division? (DOK 1)	• How can whole-number quotients of whole numbers be found? (DOK 2) • How can strategies based on place value be used to find whole-number quotients of whole numbers? (DOK 2) • How can strategies based on the properties of operations be used to find whole-number quotients of whole numbers? (DOK 2) • What is the relationship between multiplication and division? (DOK 2) • How can the relationship between multiplication and division be used to find whole-number quotients of whole numbers? (DOK 2)

Figure 8.8: How to unpack or unwrap standards to create good DOK questions.

Deliver an Inquiry-Based DOK Teaching and Learning Experience Using Good Questions

The DOK level of a good question also depends on how it's presented in an inquiry-based learning experience. Figure 8.9 (page 152) is an inquiry-based learning method and model I developed called *Inquiring Minds Map*. It shows how to develop and deliver an inquiry-based DOK teaching and learning experience using good questions that differ in their DOK levels.

The Inquiring Minds experience and process starts by asking students—or *hooking* them– with a good question. The Hook 'Em question could be any type of good question at any DOK level. For example, students can be asked a seemingly simple question such as "What is 2 + 2?" "Who was the first President of the United States?" or "What is life?" These questions would be designated a DOK 1 if they only required students to recall information or recall how to answer correctly. However, these good

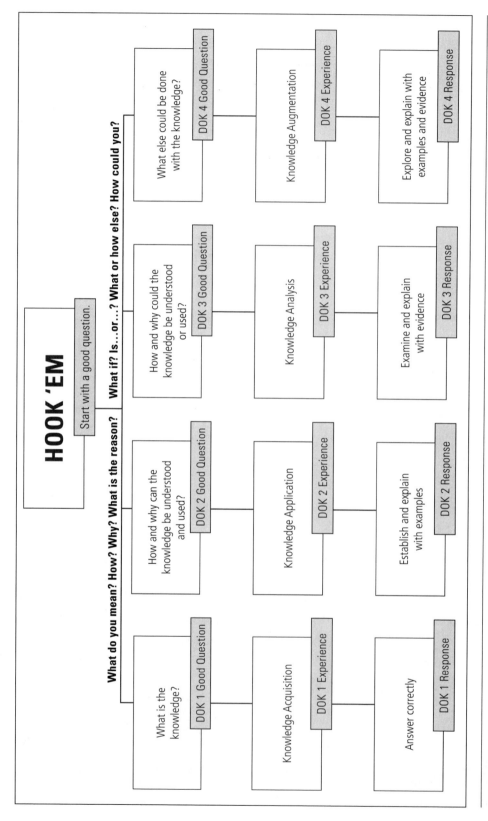

Figure 8.9: Inquiring Minds Map for Depth of Knowledge.

questions serve as the starting point for an inquiry-based DOK teaching and learning experience. Students are not required to respond or even know the answer to Hook 'Em questions—at least, not initially. They are meant to stimulate students' thinking and pique their curiosity and interest. They also necessitate students must reflect before responding.

The Hook 'Em question also introduces the good essential question that will be examined or explored and explained over the course of a comprehensive unit or an individual lesson. Figure 8.10 features four different types of good essential questions that can be used to "hook" students at the start of an inquiry-based DOK teaching and learning experience (Francis, 2016a). DOK levels vary depending on the complexity of the instructional focus and the extent of the instructional purpose. However, the intent is the same—to stimulate students' thinking, pique their curiosity and interest, and encourage them to express and share their learning.

TYPE OF ESSENTIAL QUESTION	GOOD DOK QUESTION	DOK LEVEL
Universal	What is the global or grand idea, issue, theme, or topic to be explored and explained?	DOK 1 DOK 2 DOK 3 DOK 4
Overarching	What are the core ideas and enduring understandings of a specific subject that must be established or examined and explained?	DOK 2 DOK 3
Topical	What are the instructional focus and purpose of the grade-level academic standard, activity, or assessment?	DOK 1 DOK 2 DOK 3
Driving	What could you create, design, develop, do, plan, or produce that reflects the depth of your learning?	DOK 3 DOK 4

Figure 8.10: Good essential questions to "hook 'em."

The top line of the Inquiring Minds Map features good clarifying questions that prompt students to elaborate on their responses, expand their knowledge, and extend their thinking. For example, if a student responds 4 to the good question, "What is 2 + 2?", asking "What do you mean?" will challenge students to explain how they used addition to find the sum. That's the transferrable knowledge students must develop and demonstrate. Following up the question about the first U.S. President with a good question that asks, "What if I told you there were eight people who were appointed as Presidents of the United States in Congress assembled under the Articles of Confederation?" will deepen students' knowledge, understanding, and awareness. Asking students, "How else could life be defined or explained?" after some responses are given will extend students' thinking.

The four branches of the Inquiring Minds Map show the different paths an inquiry-based DOK teaching and learning experience can take. The first row of the branch poses the good overarching question that defines and drives the demand of a specific inquiry-based DOK teaching and learning experience. The second row informs the focus and purpose of the inquiry-based DOK teaching and learning experience. The third row indicates the DOK response students must provide to the good questions asked at this branch.

Like the DOK levels, the branches are descriptors, not measures, of the different and deeper ways students can experience inquiry. They do not function like a taxonomy. An inquiry-based DOK teaching and learning experience can begin and build to any DOK level. The delivery and intensity of the inquiry depend upon the demand of the good question and the depth and extent to which students must respond.

Encourage Students to Ask Good Questions for Depth of Knowledge

Teachers should not be the only ones asking good DOK questions in class. Students should also be encouraged to ask their own questions that differ and deepen in their cognitive demand. One way to do this is to ask students what they personally want to learn about a subject. This is what I call the Good Personal Question. These good questions "motivate students to take the initiative to explore what do you want to learn about the subjects and topics being taught and then share their learning with their classmates" (Francis, 2016a, p. 21). The DOK level of these questions will vary. However, do not require students to ask a good question that will demand them to demonstrate their learning at a deeper DOK level. Also, do not direct them to change their question. The Good Personal Question is their question—the one to which they want to reflect and respond. If their question addresses the subject and meets the criteria of what a good question does, then they should be permitted to ask and address it. However, inform students that they will be expected to share what they have learned with the class.

An effective method that encourages students to ask their own good questions at different DOK levels is the Question Formulation Technique—or QFT method—developed by Dan Rothstein and Luz Santana (2011). The QFT experience begins with the teacher presenting students with the Question Focus—or QFocus—that serves as the stimulus or source of their questioning. This could be a quote, statement, image, problem, or even a standard's learning intention or target. The students are prompted to ask and write down as many questions as they can about the QFocus within a set time frame. They should not stop to discuss, critique, or even answer any of their questions. They just ask and write down questions as they come to them. Once the time is up, the students must review their questions, categorize them as open or closed, and change or revise the form or phrasing of their questions. The teacher prompts students to prioritize their questions, choosing the ones they must address first as well as the ones they believe are essential.

Using the QFT in inquiry-based DOK teaching and learning experiences involves the same process. However, after students have categorized and changed their questions, have them classify and count the type of cognitive rigor questions they have asked (for example, How many are factual, analytical, reflective, hypothetical, argumentative, or affective?). Challenge students to deepen or extend the level of Depth of Knowledge demanded by their questions. Engage students to create specific kinds of questions (for example, What kind of hypothetical question could you ask . . .?). Encourage students to be as creative and curious with their questions as possible and share the questions with the class. Provide students the opportunity to choose which questions they should address as a class or individually.

Teachers and students both asking good DOK questions deepens the demand of the DOK teaching and learning experience and fosters and promotes deeper communication and conversations between the teacher and students about the content and how it could be understood and used in different contexts. It also makes the DOK teaching and learning experience a shared one in which both the teacher and students are teaching and learning from each other.

Summary

Inquiry-based DOK teaching and learning experiences should do the following (Francis, 2016a).

- Stimulate students' thinking.
- Deepen students' knowledge, understanding, and awareness.
- Expand students' knowledge and extend their thinking.
- Pique students' curiosity, imagination, interest, and wonder.

- Encourage students to express and share their learning in their own way.

- Prompt students to reflect or research before responding.

- Phrase the goals and expectations as an interrogative statement.

These are the guidelines for teaching and learning with good questions. If the question posed prompts students to perform any of these actions, then it's a good question. However, as with the learning intention of academic standards, activities, and assessments, the DOK level of a good question depends on what comes after the question stem and the way it's used in a DOK teaching and learning experience.

Using Depth of Knowledge

Either on your own or as part of a teacher team, complete the following tasks.

Use the learning intention you deconstructed and reconstructed in chapters 5–7 or choose another one. Create good DOK questions by doing the following.

- Placing *how could you* in front of the learning intention. This will rephrase the objective statement of the learning intention as an interrogative sentence.

- Replacing the *I can* statement of the DOK learning target with *how could you*. This will rephrase the learning target statement into a good question. It's your decision whether to include the DOK skill students must perform in the good DOK question.

- Removing the DOK response students must provide in the DOK success criteria. This will rephrase the success criteria statement into a good question.

- Checking where the cognitive action verb of the learning intention is categorized in Bloom's revised taxonomy and replacing it with a question stem listed in the same level of the Bloom's inverted questioning pyramid. This will help decide the DOK response students must provide.

- Unpacking or unwrapping the standard and having the conceptual or content-specific nouns and procedural verbs set the subject of a good question that starts with one of the six Ws or the one H. These good DOK questions will prompt students to describe details and terminology or explain concepts and procedures.

Use the reproducible "From Targets to Criteria to Questions" to rephrase your DOK learning targets and DOK success criteria into good DOK questions.

From Targets to Criteria to Questions

DOK Learning Target	DOK Success Criteria	Good DOK Question

Deconstructing Depth of Knowledge: A Method and Model for Deeper Teaching and Learning
© 2022 Solution Tree Press • SolutionTree.com • Visit **go.SolutionTree.com/instruction**
to download this free reproducible.

CHAPTER NINE

Let's Make a DOK!

In 2016, I wrote a blog that compared the demand and expectations of Webb's DOK Levels to popular television shows. I called it *Let's Make a DOK!* (Francis, 2016b), a play on the title of the game show *Let's Make a Deal!* The name has a double meaning, since we can adapt the format of game shows into our classroom to develop and deliver DOK teaching and learning experiences that are not only educational but also energetic, enriching, and enjoyable.

In this chapter, you will explore how the demand of DOK teaching and learning experiences resembles the following.

- A TV quiz show such as *Jeopardy!* and *Who Wants to Be a Millionaire?* (DOK 1)

- An instructional TV show such as *The Joy of Painting with Bob Ross* and *30-Minute Meals with Rachael Ray* or a DIY video (DOK 2)

- A skills-based reality TV competition such as *Top Chef* and *LEGO Masters* or televised roundtable discussions (DOK 3)

- A business and professional reality TV show such as *Kitchen Nightmares, The Apprentice*, or *Shark Tank* (DOK 4)

You may use the experiences as described on the following pages or adapt them as needed for your classroom.

DOK 1: TV Quiz Show

The expectations of a DOK 1 teaching and learning experience are like those on a TV quiz show such as *Jeopardy!* or *Who Wants to Be a Millionaire.* On these shows, the host runs the game, provides the information, poses the questions, or presents the tasks. The questions and tasks are difficult rather than complex because they demand the contestants recall and restate or reproduce information or procedures correctly from memory. The contestant who can answer the most questions correctly or complete the most tasks successfully either wins a prize or the game.

To deliver a DOK 1 teaching and learning experience like a TV quiz show, the teacher acts as the host and poses questions or presents tasks that only require the students to answer correctly by recalling facts or demonstrating how to *just do it.* Students respond with a single word or number or a simple statement. The students pass the lesson or assessment the same way a quiz show contestant wins the game—by answering the most questions or completing the most tasks correctly or successfully. However, the goal is not for students to win but rather to be successful—and you, the teacher, will support them with achieving success. Use the quiz show analogy to help students and staff better understand their roles and responsibilities in a DOK 1 teaching and learning experience.

DOK 2: Instructional TV Shows and DIY Videos

To better understand the difference between a DOK 1 and a DOK 2 teaching and learning experience, watch a clip from an instructional TV show such as *The Joy of Painting with Bob Ross* or *30-Minute Meals with Rachael Ray.* These shows are DOK 2s because the star of each show not only shows but also shares how they understand and can use the knowledge of how to paint a spectacular landscape scene or prepare a delicious meal in no more than thirty minutes. However, when the volume is muted or turned down, it's a DOK 1 because they are only *demonstrating* how to do something. That's the key difference between a DOK 1 and DOK 2 teaching and learning experience. Students must communicate *and* demonstrate how and why they understand and can use mental processing. This allows the student to shift their role from the learner, who recalls and restates or reproduces, to the teacher, who shows and shares or summarizes.

Inform students in a DOK 2 teaching and learning experience that they are the star of the show. The camera or spotlight is on them to show and share or summarize how they can use the subject-specific knowledge and skills accurately to accomplish a specific activity, item, or task. You, the teacher, are the producer or director of the show who will guide the students' performance by prompting them continuously to describe and explain how and why. The success of the student's performance or show is based not only on whether they complete the task correctly but also how clearly they communicate ideas, processes, or reasoning. To make a DOK 2 teaching and learning experience more creative and enjoyable, you could also have your students produce their own do-it-yourself (DIY) videos starring them explaining how they understand or can use the mental processing they have acquired and developed.

DOK 3: Skills-Based Reality TV Competitions and Roundtable Discussions

The expectations of DOK 3 teaching and learning experiences are like skills-based reality TV competitions such as *Top Chef* or *LEGO Masters*. These shows place participants in a controlled situation or simulation of a real-world experience that engages them to think strategically about how they could understand and use their knowledge to accomplish a complex task or produce a creative or original product within a certain timeframe using the resources or tools available to them. However, what distinguishes reality TV competition shows is that the competitors must justify their actions, decisions, or reasoning continuously throughout the experience, be it to the host, the judges evaluating them, or even to the audience. The competitors' success depends not only on whether they accomplish the goal but also on whether they can convey to others their actions, decisions, and reasoning, and convince others that their actions, decisions, and reasoning are credible and valid given the situation and stipulations.

To deliver a DOK 3 teaching and learning experience like a reality TV competition show, present the students with a common goal they must achieve within a specific timeframe and using certain ingredients or tools. It could be a task they must accomplish or a product they must produce. That's the answer. Put the question stem "How could you . . . ?" in front of the goal statement or the objective of the task. That's the good driving question students must address. Allow the students to choose to work collaboratively or independently to achieve the goal. Like the host of a reality TV competition show, walk the room monitoring the experience and informing students of how much time they have to complete the task or produce the product. Ask probing questions students must justify and hypothetical questions to consider. Once time is up, have students present their product or share their experience, explaining and justifying their actions, decisions, or reasoning with evidentiary support. Their presentation must not only explain how they accomplished the goal but also why they tackled the task or produced the product as they did. Inform the students they will be evaluated not only on whether they were able to complete the task or product successfully but also how clearly and convincingly they can explain their ideas, processes, and reasoning with credible evidentiary support.

DOK 3 teaching and learning experiences can also be roundtable discussions similar to segments featured on TV political programs such as *Meet the Press*, talk shows such as *The View*, or sports highlight shows such as *Inside the NFL*. Each of these shows features a segment in which the host presents a topic or poses a question and moderates the conversation between the participants. The participants engage in deep dialogues or debates in which they not only explain but also justify their analysis or evaluation of a situation by drawing upon their deep knowledge or understanding and using evidentiary reasoning to strengthen and support their claims or commentary. The host and participants push the conversations deeper and further through a combination of shared dialogue and inquiry driven by good open-ended questions that not only stimulate deeper thinking but encourage deeper discussions.

To deliver a DOK 3 teaching and learning experience that resembles a roundtable segment on a political, talk, or sports TV show, pose an open-ended good question about the text or topic you are reading or reviewing in class. Inform the students they are not required to answer the question correctly. However, they must address the question by examining and explaining in-depth the ideas presented in the text or issues pertaining to the topic. The conversations between students may waver between a DOK 2 and a DOK 3 as students use examples or evidence to strengthen and support their commentary—and that's OK! However, engage students to defend or refute with evidence why their examples are accurate, reasonable, or valid. These roundtable segments can be moderated with the whole class or organized into small groups in which the students engage in their own discussions and share their claims, conclusions, and conjectures with the class to foster deeper dialogues or fuel further debates.

DOK 4: Business and Professional Reality TV Shows

DOK 4 teaching and learning experiences can resemble reality TV business and professional shows such as *Kitchen Nightmares*, *The Apprentice*, and *Shark Tank*. These TV shows are problem-based and project-based learning experiences that demand entrepreneurs and experts to think extensively about how they could understand and use their personal expertise to address a problem or accomplish a project. In some situations, the problems and projects can be so wicked or impossible that they cannot be completed or solved successfully despite the entrepreneur or expert's best efforts. However, these shows document the real struggles and successes of the world of work.

Kitchen Nightmares is a problem-based learning experience—specifically, a wicked problem-based learning experience. On this show, Gordon Ramsay, an expert chef and restauranteur, is called in by a restaurant owner to help them restructure or revive a struggling or failing dining establishment. Most of the episodes of *Kitchen Nightmares* end on a positive note with the struggling or failing restaurant experiencing a successful turnaround. However, in many cases, the solution is mostly a quick fix only suitable for the given situation. In fact, according to an article published by Joanna Fantozzi and Debra Kelly (2020), "15 restaurants out of the 77 that appeared on the show between 2007 and 2014 are still open." The failure rate cannot be attributed solely to Ramsay, who was called in to provide consultation and share his personal expertise. Opening and operating a restaurant (or, indeed, any business) is a wicked problem due to the myriad of factors and issues involved—most of them unpredictable and even volatile. There's no specific formula or process for running a successful business. All struggling or failing businesses like the ones on *Kitchen Nightmares* can do is call in those with personal expertise to address the problem when it becomes too overwhelming—or wicked. However, there are no guarantees the solutions suggested by the expert will work—or even last.

DOK 4 teaching and learning experiences resembling *Kitchen Nightmares* extend the expert thinking students developed and demonstrated at the DOK 3 level. The students are called in individually or as a group to address an extremely complex real-world issue or problem. It doesn't have to be a wicked problem or impossible project. However, it should extend students' learning over a period of time and take them beyond the confines of the content, the curriculum, or the classroom (if they must address the problem or accomplish the task within a set period of time in the classroom, it's a DOK 3). The students follow a problem-based learning process and draw upon the disciplinary literacies and core competencies they have developed to address the problem or accomplish the task. The students present their conclusions, recommendations, or solutions supported with relevant examples and evidence. Student performance should be assessed not only on the success of the solution but on how effectively they addressed the issue or situation using problem-solving methods and strategies. Students should conduct a self-evaluation of their performance.

The Apprentice is a project-based learning experience. On this show, the participants are "candidates" with diverse personal expertise who are organized into teams—which the showrunners call "corporations"—that must address an intricate problem or accomplish an involved project. The episodes show the trials and tribulations of each candidate and corporation as they attempt to develop a plan or design a product that addresses the problem presented or project assigned. The plan or product, the process for design and development, and the performance of the corporation and its individual members are all evaluated by the host, their advisors, and the members of each team. This all takes place in the boardroom, where the candidates not only have to explain their plan, product, and process but also justify their actions, decisions, and results so they won't be eliminated from the competition.

To deliver a DOK 4 teaching and learning experience that resembles *The Apprentice*, organize your students into groups or teams. Present them with a problem they must address or a project they must accomplish. As with the *Kitchen Nightmares* DOK 4 teaching and learning experience, the problem or project doesn't have to be a wicked problem or impossible project. However, it should extend students' learning over a period of time and take them beyond the confines of the content, the curriculum, or the classroom (if they must address the problem or accomplish the task within a set period of time in the classroom, it's a DOK 3). They should document the process and their experience—be it in print or visually—of addressing the problem or accomplishing the project. At the end of the experience, have the students present the plan or product to a panel of representatives or stakeholders from the school (for example, teachers, site or district administrators, or members of the community) or those who will be affected by the plan or product. Student presentations should explain the purpose of their project, detail their planning and production process, and justify their actions and decisions. The success of the plan, the product, and the students' performance should be evaluated by the stakeholder reviewers. Students should also conduct a self-evaluation and an evaluation of their peers in which they critique and justify their performance with examples and evidence.

Shark Tank is an authentic learning experience that features individuals who use their personal expertise to address a problem or accomplish a project by developing a plan or designing a product. On *Shark Tank*, aspiring entrepreneurs and inventors pitch their company or product to a panel of investors—the "sharks"—with the hopes of landing a deal and establishing a business partnership. *Shark Tank* is as much about the pitch as it is about the project. The success of a *Shark Tank* pitch is based not only on the quality of the proposal plan or product but also the presentation. The question is twofold—what kind of innovative plan or inventive product could the entrepreneur or inventor come up with, and how could they convince the "sharks" that their idea or invention is a worthwhile investment?

DOK 4 teaching and learning experiences based on *Shark Tank* are not only extremely extensive but also highly personalized. Instead of assigning a specific problem or accomplishing a project they must address and accomplish, students are encouraged to explore and explain with examples and evidence how they could use their personal expertise to address a problem or accomplish a project of their own choice. They are also encouraged to think extensively about how they could develop or design an original plan or product. Like the DOK 4 *The Apprentice* teaching and learning experience, the students should present the plan or product to a panel of evaluators. However, student presentations should be evaluated based on the quality of the pitch, not the process or even the plan or product. The goal is for the students to use extended reasoning supported by examples and evidence to convince the evaluators that their plan or product has quality, is worthwhile or long lasting, or has the potential to be something greater.

Summary

Of all the ways I have explained Depth of Knowledge and Webb's DOK levels, the TV show analogy makes the most sense to both teachers and administrators. In fact, I use the TV show analogies so instructional leaders and coaches who work with teachers can understand what teaching and learning for Depth of Knowledge looks like in a classroom at any grade level in any subject. Comparing the learning goals and expectations of a DOK teaching and learning experience to the objectives of popular TV shows makes Depth of Knowledge and the DOK levels feel more accessible, applicable, and even amusing.

Using Depth of Knowledge

Either on your own or as part of a teacher team, complete the following tasks.

Plan and provide a DOK teaching and learning experience that resembles one of the following television show formats.

- A quiz show that requires contestants to recall information or recall how to do something to answer correctly. That's a DOK 1.

- An instructional how-to video or program that features someone demonstrating and communicating how to apply knowledge, concepts, or skills or use information and basic reasoning to answer a question, address a problem, accomplish a task, or analyze a specific text or topic. That's a DOK 2.

- A reality competition in which contestants think strategically to examine and explain with evidence how they could use their knowledge or skills to accomplish a complex activity or task within a given timeframe. That's a DOK 3.

- A roundtable show in which participants use complex reasoning supported by evidence to engage in a debate or discussion about a text or a topic. That's also a DOK 3.

- A business reality show that encourages an individual or group to use extended reasoning supported by expertise or to think extensively about how they could address, explain, or respond to a real-world scenario or situation insightfully, innovatively, inventively, or in their own unique way. That's a DOK 4.

EPILOGUE

Depth of Knowledge is a complex, confusing, and even contentious concept. This is not just because we were provided with an inaccurate resource and tool with the DOK wheel, it's also because Depth of Knowledge demands us to look at teaching and learning differently.

What you've read in this book is my interpretation of Depth of Knowledge and my ideas of how the DOK levels can be used as a method and model that inform how teaching and learning experiences can be developed, delivered, and deepened. My interpretation is based on years of reading, researching, and reviewing both Norman L. Webb's paper on standards and assessment alignment and Karin Hess's work with cognitive rigor. It's also based on my own experience working with educators around the world sharing the truth about the DOK wheel and showing them how the DOK levels could be used as a multitiered system of supports to deliver instruction, respond to intervention, extend learning, and make modifications. It also emphasizes and supports what Hess (2013a) says about Depth of Knowledge:

> The task or objective's central verb(s) alone is/are not sufficient to assign a DOK level. [Educators] must consider 'what comes after verb'—the complexity of the task and content/concepts—in addition to the mental processing required by the requirements set forth in the objective. (p. 5)

This is the core idea and enduring understanding of Depth of Knowledge. It's also what you need to keep in mind when planning and providing a DOK teaching and learning experience. When determining Depth of Knowledge demanded by an academic standard, activity, or assessment, ask yourself the following.

- "What exactly must students learn?"

- "How deeply must students understand and use their learning?"

Once you know this, then you can designate the level of Depth of Knowledge required according to the DOK levels based on the demand of the following.

- The DOK task students must complete

- The DOK skill students must perform

- The DOK response students must provide

These DOK descriptors can be used to check and confirm the consistency between academic standards and the activities and assessments that address them. They can also be used to construct the DOK learning targets and clarify the DOK success criteria students must achieve and surpass to demonstrate proficiency, perform successfully, and progress in their learning. Those learning targets and success criteria can also be rephrased into good questions that can be used to develop and deliver DOK teaching and learning experiences that are inquiry-based. Those inquiry-based DOK teaching and learning experiences can also resemble popular TV shows that demand their participants demonstrate their learning over a range of DOK levels.

Figure E.1 provides a comprehensive overview and summary of the key ideas and strategies addressed in this book. The information in this table comes from Webb's research on alignment studies, Dr. Karin Hess's work with cognitive rigor, and my own ideas and strategies on how the DOK levels can be used as a method and model that inform how teaching and learning experiences can be developed, delivered, and deepened.

The level of Depth of Knowledge demanded by a DOK teaching and learning experience depends on the demand of the standard and the strengths of the student. However, it's your discretion as the teacher to decide the delivery and intensity of the instruction. You can adapt or adjust the DOK level to whatever level is needed to guide and support your students to achieve and surpass both the proficiency goals and expectations set by the standards and personal goals and expectations students set for themselves. In fact, I encourage you to think critically and creatively about how you could make Depth of Knowledge and Webb's DOK levels work for both you and your students. The non-negotiables, however, are as follows.

- Depth of Knowledge is based on the complexity of the content knowledge students must learn and the depth and extent to which students must understand and use their learning in a certain context, not the cognitive action students perform.

- Depth of Knowledge requires looking beyond the cognitive action verb at the words that identify the instructional focus and inform the instructional purpose. Those words and phrases will determine the

LEVEL	FOCUS	COGNITIVE DEMAND	LEARNING EXPERIENCE	DOK TASK	DOK SKILL	DOK RESPONSE	DOK IT	GOOD DOK QUESTION
DOK 1	Recall and restate or reproduce	Low	Knowledge acquisition	Just the facts Just do it	Recall information Recall how to	Answer correctly	Answer it	What is the knowledge?
DOK 2	Concepts, skills, and basic reasoning	Moderate	Knowledge application	Show and share or summarize Comprehend and communicate Specify and explain Give examples and non-examples	Apply knowledge, concepts, and skills Use information and basic reasoning	Establish and explain with examples	Use it to explain it	How and why can the knowledge be understood and used?
DOK 3	Strategic thinking and complex reasoning	High	Knowledge analysis	Delve deeper Inquire and investigate Critical thinking and problem solving Creative thinking Defend, justify, or refute with evidence Connect, confirm, consider, conclude, or critique	Think strategically Use complex reasoning with evidence	Examine and explain with evidence	Use it to prove it	How and why could the knowledge be understood and used?
DOK 4	Extended thinking and reasoning	Extensive	Knowledge augmentation	Go deep within a subject area Go among texts and topics Go across the curriculum Go beyond the classroom	Use extended reasoning supported by expertise Think extensively	Explore and explain with examples and evidence (over an extended period of time)	Go for it	What else could be done with the knowledge?

Sources: Florida Department of Education, 2008; Francis, 2016a; Webb, 1999.

Figure E.1: What is Depth of Knowledge?

demand of the DOK task students must complete, the DOK skill students must perform, and the DOK response students must provide.

- Depth of Knowledge describes the cognitive demand of academic standards, curricular activities, and test items, not their level of difficulty. Difficult activities, items, and tasks are easy or hard. Demanding teaching and learning expectations and experiences are simple, complex, or involved.

- The DOK levels categorize and describe four different and deeper ways students can understand and use the content knowledge in certain contexts; it's not a taxonomy that builds upon or scaffolds levels of teaching and learning. However, it could be used as a multitiered system of support to deliver instruction, respond to intervention, extend learning, and make modifications.

- DOK teaching and learning experiences are both standards-based and student-centered. Teaching and testing for Depth of Knowledge start and stop with the standards. However, teaching and learning for Depth of Knowledge tier to the level of Depth of Knowledge students can perform successfully and build upon their strengths and successes so they can rise to, reach, and go beyond the DOK level of the standard's learning intention.

- The direction of a DOK teaching and learning experience depends on the demand of the standard, the delivery and intensity of instruction, and the strengths of the student.

- Depth of Knowledge demands us to ask two questions when clarifying and confirming the cognitive demand of a teaching and learning experience: what exactly and how deeply?

Knowing this will help you plan and provide a DOK teaching and learning experience that will be academically rigorous, socially and emotionally supportive, and student responsive.

REFERENCES AND RESOURCES

Ainsworth, L. (2003). *"Unwrapping" the standards: A simple process to make standards manageable.* Denver, CO: Advanced Learning Press.

Anderson, L. W., & Krathwohl, D. (Eds.). (2001). *A taxonomy for learning, teaching, and assessing: A revision of Bloom's taxonomy of educational objectives.* New York: Addison Wesley Longman.

Bentley, J., & Toth, M. (2020). *Exploring wicked problems: What they are and why they are important.* Bloomington, IN: Archway Publishing.

Berger, R., Rugen, L., & Woodfin, L. (2014). *Leaders of their own learning: Transforming schools through student-engaged assessment.* San Francisco: Jossey-Bass.

Biggs, J. B., & Collis, K. F. (1982). *Evaluating the quality of learning: The SOLO taxonomy (Structure of the Observed Learning Outcome).* New York: Academic Press.

Blackburn, B. R. (2013). *Rigor is NOT a four-letter word* (2nd ed.). Larchmont, NY: Eye on Education.

Blackburn, B. R., & Witzel, B. S. (2018). *Rigor in the RTI and MTSS classroom: Practical tools and strategies.* New York: Routledge.

Bloom, B. (1956). *Taxonomy of educational objectives, handbook I: The cognitive domain.* New York: David McKay.

Buffum, A., Mattos, M., & Malone, J. (2018). *Taking action: A handbook for RTI at Work.* Bloomington, IN: Solution Tree Press.

Buffum, A., Mattos, M., & Weber, C. (2009). *Pyramid response to intervention: RTI, professional learning communities, and how to respond when kids don't learn.* Bloomington, IN: Solution Tree Press.

Cash, R. M. (2017). *Advancing differentiation: Thinking and learning for the 21st century* (Rev. ed.). Minneapolis, MN: Free Spirit Publishing.

Chauvin, R., & Theodore, K. (2015). Teaching content-area literacy and disciplinary literacy. *SEDL Insights, 3*(1). Accessed at https://sedl.org/insights/3-1/teaching _content_area_literacy_and_disciplinary_literacy.pdf on June 1, 2021.

Clark, B. (1983). *Growing up gifted: Developing the potential of children at home and at school* (2nd ed.). Columbus, OH: Charles E. Merrill.

Clapton, E., & Robertson, R. (1986). It's in the way that you use it. *August* [CD]. Burbank, CA: Warner Bros.

Conklin, J. E. (2006). *Dialogue mapping: Building a shared understanding of wicked problems.* Hoboken, NJ: John Wiley & Sons.

Cook, H. G. (2005, December 21). *Alignment Report 6: Aligning English language proficiency tests to English language learning standards—Aligning assessment to guide the learning of all students.* Washington, DC: Council of Chief State School Officers. Accessed at https://citeseerx.ist.psu.edu/viewdoc/download?doi=10.1.1.465 .7548&rep=rep1&type=pdf on July 10, 2021.

Cook, H. G. (2007). *Some thoughts on English language proficiency standards to academic content standards alignment.* Madison: Wisconsin Center for Education Research. Accessed at www.nciea.org/publications /RILS_3_GC07.pdf on July 10, 2021.

Costa, A. L., & Kallick, B. (Eds.). (2008). *Learning and leading with habits of mind: 16 essential characteristics for success.* Alexandria, VA: Association for Supervision and Curriculum Development.

Council of Chief State School Officers. (2012). *Common Core State Standards.* Washington, DC: Author.

Council of Chief State School Officers. (2014). *English language proficiency (ELP) standards.* Washington, DC: Author.

Department of Education, Skills, and Employment. (2015). Humanities and social sciences: Civics and citizenship—Year 8—Foundation—year 10 Australian curriculum. Sydney, Australia: Author. Accessed at www.australiancurriculum.edu.au /Search/?q=ACHCK064 on July 11, 2021.

Dobson, M. S. (2013). *Project: Impossible—How the great leaders of history identified, solved, and accomplished the seemingly impossible—and how you can too!* Oshawa, Ontario: Multi-Media Publications.

DuFour, R., & DuFour, R. (2012). *Essentials for principals: The school leader's guide to Professional Learning Communities at Work.* Bloomington, IN: Solution Tree Press.

DuFour, R., DuFour, R., Eaker, R., Many, T. W., & Mattos, M. (2016). *Learning by doing: A handbook for Professional Learning Communities at Work.* (3rd ed.). Bloomington, IN: Solution Tree Press.

DuFour, R., & Eaker, R. (1998). *Professional Learning Communities at Work: Best practices for enhancing student achievement.* Bloomington, IN: Solution Tree Press.

Dweck, C. S. (2006). *Mindset: The new psychology of success.* New York: Random House.

Englehardt, M. D., Furst, E. J., Hill, W. H., & Krathwohl, D. R. (1956). In B. S. Bloom (Ed.), *Taxonomy of educational objectives: The classification of educational goals, handbook 1—Cognitive domain.* New York: David McKay.

Fantozzi, J., & Kelly, D. (2020, May 18). *The untold truth of kitchen nightmares* [Blog post]. Accessed at www.mashed.com/121110/untold-truth-kitchen-nightmares on March 24, 2021.

Fink, L. D. (2013). *Creating significant learning experiences: An integrated approach to designing college courses.* San Francisco: Jossey-Bass.

Florida Department of Education. (2008). *Cognitive complexity/depth of knowledge rating.* Accessed at https://backend.cpalms.org/textonly.aspx?ContentID=23&UrlPath=/page23.aspx on July 17, 2021.

Francis, E. M. (2016a). *Now that's a good question! How to promote cognitive rigor through classroom questioning.* Alexandria, VA: Association for Supervision and Curriculum Development.

Francis, E. M. (2016b, September). *Let's make a D.O.K.! A game show analogy to Depth of Knowledge* [Blog post]. Accessed at http://inservice.ascd.org/lets-make-a-d-o-k-a-game-show-analogy-to-Depth-of-Knowledge on March 24, 2021.

Francis, E. M. (2016c, August). *Why the D. O. K. wheel does not address Depth of Knowledge* [Blog post]. Accessed at http://inservice.ascd.org/why-the-d-o-k-wheel-does-not-address-Depth-of-Knowledge on March 24, 2021.

Francis, E. M. (2017, May). *What is Depth of Knowledge?* Accessed at http://inservice.ascd.org/what-exactly-is-Depth-of-Knowledge-hint-its-not-a-wheel on March 24, 2021.

Gillis, V. (2014). Disciplinary literacy: Adapt not adopt. *Journal of Adolescent and Adult Literacy, 57*(8), 613–623.

Hattie, J. A. C. (2009). *Visible learning: A synthesis of over 800 meta-analyses relating to achievement.* New York: Routledge.

Hattie, J. (2012). *Visible learning for teachers: Maximizing impact on learning.* New York: Routledge.

Hess, K. J. (2005a). *Applying Webb's depth of knowledge levels in writing* [White paper]. Dover, NH: Center for Assessment. Accessed at www.nciea.org/publications/DOKwriting_KH08.pdf on March 6, 2021.

Hess, K. J. (2005b). *Applying Webb's depth of knowledge levels in social studies* [White paper]. Dover, NH: Center for Assessment. Accessed at www.nciea.org/publications/DOKsocialstudies_KH08.pdf on March 6, 2021.

Hess, K. J. (2006). *Exploring cognitive demand in instruction and assessment.* Dover, NH: National Center for Assessment.

Hess, K. J. (2010a). *Applying Webb's depth of knowledge levels in science* [White paper]. Dover, NH: Center for Assessment.

Hess, K. J. (2010b). *Hess cognitive rigor matrix | Health and physical education CRM.* Accessed at www.karin-hess.com/free-resources on March 25, 2021.

Hess, K. J. (2013a). *Linking research with practice: A local assessment toolkit to guide school leaders.* Underhill, VT: Educational Research in Action.

Hess, K. J. (2013b). *A guide for using Webb's Depth of Knowledge with Common Core State Standards.* New York: Common Core Institute.

Hess, K. J. (2013c). *Hess cognitive rigor matrix | Math-science CRM.* Accessed at www.karin-hess.com/free-resources on March 25, 2021.

Hess, K. J. (2013d). *Hess cognitive rigor matrix | Reading-listening CRM.* Accessed at www.karin-hess.com/free-resources on March 25, 2021.

Hess, K. J. (2013e). *Hess cognitive rigor matrix | Writing-speaking CRM.* Accessed at www.karin-hess.com/free-resources on March 25, 2021.

Hess, K. J. (2013f). *Hess cognitive rigor matrix | Social studies-humanities CRM.* Accessed at www.karin-hess.com/free-resources on March 25, 2021.

Hess, K. J. (2013g). *Hess cognitive rigor matrix | Fine arts CRM.* Accessed at www.karin-hess.com/free-resources on March 25, 2021.

Hess, K. J. (2015). *Hess cognitive rigor matrix | World languages CRM.* Accessed at www.karin-hess.com/free-resources on March 25, 2021.

Hess, K. J. (2017). *Hess cognitive rigor matrix | Career and technical education (CTE) CRM.* Accessed at www.karin-hess.com/free-resources on March 25, 2021.

Hess, K. J. (2018). *A local assessment toolkit to promote deeper learning: Transforming research into practice.* Thousand Oaks, CA: Corwin Press.

Hess, K. J., Carlock, D., Jones, B., & Walkup, J. R. (2009a, March 7). *Cognitive rigor: Blending the strengths of Bloom's Taxonomy and Webb's Depth of Knowledge to enhance classroom-level processes.* Accessed at https://files.eric.ed.gov/fulltext/ED517804.pdf on June 1, 2021.

Hess, K. J., Carlock, D., Jones, B., & Walkup, J. R. (2009b, June). *What exactly do "fewer, clearer, and higher standards" really look like in the classroom? Using a cognitive rigor matrix to analyze curriculum, plan lessons, and implement assessments.* Accessed at www.nciea.org/publications/cognitiverigorpaper_KH12.pdf on July 10, 2021.

Hess, K. J., Colby, R. L., & Joseph, D. A. (2020). *Deeper competency-based learning: Making equitable, student-centered, sustainable shifts.* Thousand Oaks, CA: Corwin Press.

Jonassen, D. H. (2011). *Learning to solve problems: A handbook for designing problem-solving learning environments.* New York: Routledge.

Kolko, J. (2012). *Wicked problems: Problems worth solving—A handbook & call to action.* Austin, TX: Austin Center for Design.

Krathwohl, D. R., Bloom, B. S., & Masia, B. B. (1964). *Taxonomy of educational objectives: The classification of educational goals. Handbook II: Affective domain.* New York: Longman.

Mager, R. F. (1997). *Preparing instructional objectives: A critical tool in the development of effective instruction* (3rd ed.). Atlanta, GA: Center for Effective Performance.

Marzano, R. J., & Kendall, J. S. (2007). *The new taxonomy of educational objectives.* Thousand Oaks, CA: Corwin Press.

Marzano, R. J., Rogers, K., & Simms, J. A. (2015). *Vocabulary for the new science standards.* Bloomington, IN: Marzano Resources.

Marzano, R. J., & Simms, J. A. (2013). *Vocabulary for the Common Core.* Bloomington, IN: Marzano Research Laboratory.

Mattos, M., DuFour, R., DuFour, R., Eaker, R., & Many, T. W. (2016). *Concise answers to frequently asked questions about Professional Learning Communities at Work.* Bloomington, IN: Solution Tree Press.

McKnight, K. S. (2019). *Literacy & learning centers for the big kids: Building literacy skills and content knowledge for grades 4–12* (2nd ed.). Antioch, IL: Engaging Learners.

Merrotsy, P. (2008). Acceleration. In N. J. Salkind (Ed.), *Encyclopedia of educational psychology.* Thousand Oaks, CA: SAGE.

Miller, B. (n.d.). *The purpose of project management and setting objectives* [Blog post]. Accessed at www.projectsmart.co.uk/purpose-of-project-management-and-setting -objectives.php on March 25, 2021.

Miller, G. A. (1956). The magical number seven, plus or minus two: Some limits on our capacity for processing information. *Psychological Review, 63*(2), 81–97.

Ministry of Education Singapore. (2021). *Lower secondary express course/normal (academic) course: History teaching and learning syllabuses. History teaching and learning syllabuses.* Singapore: Curriculum and Planning Development Division. Accessed at www.moe .gov.sg/-/media/files/secondary/syllabuses/humanities/2021-history-lower-secondary -syllabus.pdf?la=en&hash=9D281C8101FE82CB29FD1C4754E37AB3FBEB1945 on July 14, 2021.

Moore, C., Garst, L. H., & Marzano, R. J. (2015). *Creating & using learning targets & performance scales: How teachers make better instructional decisions.* Blairsville, PA: Learning Sciences International.

Moss, C., & Brookhart, S. (2012). *Learning targets: Helping students aim for understanding in today's lesson.* Alexandria, VA: Association for Supervision and Curriculum Development.

National Center for History in the Schools. (1996). *National standards for history basic edition.* Los Angeles: UCLA Public History Initiative. Accessed at https://phi.history .ucla.edu/nchs/history-standards on March 25, 2021.

National Council for the Social Studies. (2013). *The College, Career, and Civic Life (C3) Framework for Social Studies State Standards: Guidance for enhancing the rigor of K–12 civics, economics, geography, and history.* Silver Spring, MD: Author.

National Council of Teachers of Mathematics. (2000). *Principles and standards for school mathematics*. Reston, VA: Author.

National Governors Association Center for Best Practices & Council of Chief State School Officers. (2010a). *Mathematics standards*. Washington, DC: Authors. Accessed at www.corestandards.org/Math on July 6, 2021.

National Governors Association Center for Best Practices & Council of Chief State School Officers. (2010b). *English language arts standards*. Washington, DC: Authors. Accessed at www.corestandards.org/ELA-Literacy on July 6, 2021.

New York City Department of Education Promising Practice Plus. (n.d.). *Introduction to depth of knowledge* [Video file]. Accessed at www.weteachnyc.org/resources/resource /introduction-depth-knowledge/?collection_id=22 on July 17, 2021.

NGSS Lead States. (2013). *Next Generation Science Standards: For states, by states*. Washington, DC: National Academies Press.

Ontario Ministry of Education. (2007). *The Ontario curriculum grades 1-8: Science and technology*. Toronto, Ontario, CAN: Author. Accessed at www.edu.gov.on.ca/eng /curriculum/elementary/scientec18currb.pdf on July 11, 2021.

Partnership for 21st Century Learning. (2019). *Framework for 21st Century Learning: Definitions*. Hilliard, OH: Battelle for Kids. Accessed at http://static.battelleforkids .org/documents/p21/P21_Framework_DefinitionsBFK.pdf on July 13, 2021.

Patterson, L. G., Musselman, M., & Rowlet, J. (2013). Using the depth of knowledge model to create high school mathematics assessments—RESEARCH. *Kentucky Journal of Excellence in College Teaching and Learning, 11*(4), 39–45.

Petit, M., & Hess, K. (2006). *Applying Webb's Depth-of-Knowledge (DOK) and NAEP levels of complexity in mathematics*. Dover, NH: National Center for Assessment. Accessed at www.nciea.org/publications/DOKmath_KH08.pdf on October 12, 2021.

Pink, D. H. (2009). *Drive: The surprising truth about what motivates us*. New York: Riverhead Books.

Project AERO. (2018). *AERO world language standards and benchmarks*. Accessed at www .projectaero.org/AEROplus/languages/AERO_world_language_standards.pdf on March 25, 2021.

Renzulli, J. S., & Reis, S. M. (2014). *The schoolwide enrichment model: A how-to guide for talent development* (3rd ed.). Waco, TX: Prufrock Press.

Rittel, H. W. J., & Webber, M. M. (1973). Dilemmas in a general theory of planning. *Policy Sciences, 4*, 155–169.

Rothstein, D., & Santana, L. (2011). *Make just one change: Teach students to ask their own questions*. Cambridge, MA: Harvard Education Press.

Shanahan, T., & Shanahan, C. (2008). Teaching disciplinary literacy to adolescents: Rethinking content-area literacy. *Harvard Educational Review, 78*(1), 40–59.

Shanahan, T., & Shanahan, C. (2012). What is disciplinary literacy and why does it matter? *Top Language Disorders, 32*(1), 7–18.

SHAPE America. (2013). *Grade-level outcomes for K–12 physical education.* Reston, VA: Author. Accessed at www.shapeamerica.org/standards/pe/upload/Grade-Level -Outcomes-for-K-12-Physical-Education.pdf on August 23, 2021.

Sousa, D. A. (2011). *How the brain learns* (4th ed.). Thousand Oaks, CA: Corwin Press.

State Education Agency Directors of Arts Education. (2014). *National Core Arts Standards.* Dover, DE: State Education Agency Directors of Arts Education. Accessed at www.nationalartsstandards.org/ on July 6, 2021.

Stein, M. K., Smith, M. S., Henningsen, M. A., & Silver, E. A. (2000). *Implementing standards-based mathematics instruction: A casebook for professional development.* New York: Teachers College Press.

Texas Education Agency. (2011). *Texas Essential Knowledge and Skills.* Accessed at https:// tea.texas.gov/academics/curriculum-standards/teks/texas-essential-knowledge-and -skills on March 25, 2021.

Tienken, C. (2016, June 28). *Don't be fooled: Complexity versus difficulty* [Blog post]. Accessed at https://christienken.com/2016/06/28/dont-be-fooled-complexity-versus -difficulty on March 25, 2021.

Tindal, G. (2005). *Alignment Report 2: Alignment of alternate assessments using the Webb system—Aligning assessment to guide the learning of all students.* Washington, DC: Council of Chief State School Officers. Accessed at https://citeseerx.ist.psu.edu /viewdoc/download?doi=10.1.1.465.7548&rep=rep1&type=pdf on July 10, 2021.

Trilling, B., & Fadel, C. (2009). *21st century skills: Learning and life for our times.* San Francisco: Jossey-Bass.

Walkup, J. R. (2013, December 24). *Bad DOK chart sabotages understanding of depth of knowledge* [Blog post]. Accessed at http://cognitiverigor.blogspot.com/2014/04 /by-john-r.html on March 25, 2021.

Walkup, J. R. (2014, January 24). *Karin Hess weighs in on bad depth of knowledge (DOK) chart* [Blog post]. Accessed at http://cognitiverigor.blogspot.com/2014/04/karin-hess- weighs-in-on-bad-depth-of.html on March 25, 2021.

Walkup, J. R. (2020). *The art and science of lesson design: Practical approaches to boosting cognitive rigor in the classroom.* Lanham, MD: Rowman & Littlefield.

Webb, N. L. (1997). *Criteria for alignment of expectations and assessments on mathematics and science education* (Research Monograph No. 6). Madison, WI: National Institute for Science Education. Accessed at https://files.eric.ed.gov/fulltext/ED414305.pdf on March 6, 2021.

Webb, N. L. (1999). *Alignment of science and mathematics standards and assessment in four states* (Research Monograph No. 18). Madison, WI: National Institute for Science

Education. Accessed at https://files.eric.ed.gov/fulltext/ED440852.pdf on March 6, 2021.

Webb, N. L. (2002, March 28). *Depth of Knowledge levels for four content areas* [White paper]. Accessed at http://apps.web.maine.gov/doe/sites/maine.gov.doe/files/inline-files/dok.pdf on July 16, 2021.

Webb, N. L. (2005, July). *Web alignment tool (WAT): Training manual.* Madison, WI: University of Wisconsin. Accessed at http://watv2.wceruw.org/Training%20Manual%202.1%20Draft%20091205.doc on March 6, 2021.

Webb, N. L. (2007). Issues related to judging the alignment of curriculum standards and assessments. *Applied Measurement in Education, 20*(1), 7–25.

Webb, N. L. (2008a, June 28). *Alignment analysis of reading extended grade band standards and assessments: Wisconsin, grades 3–8 and 10.* Madison, WI: Wisconsin Department of Public Instruction. Accessed at https://dpi.wi.gov/sites/default/files/imce/assessment/pdf/tdwaa-2008-readpostrpt.pdf on March 6, 2021.

Webb, N. L. (2008b, June 28). *Alignment analysis of mathematics extended grade band standards and assessments: Wisconsin, grades 3–8 and 10.* Madison, WI: Wisconsin Department of Public Instruction. Accessed at https://dpi.wi.gov/sites/default/files/imce/assessment/pdf/tdwaa-2008-mathpostrpt.pdf on March 6, 2021.

Webb, N. L. (2008c, June 28). *Alignment analysis of science extended grade band standards and assessments: Wisconsin grades 4, 8 and 10.* Madison, WI: Wisconsin Department of Public Instruction. Accessed at https://dpi.wi.gov/sites/default/files/imce/assessment/pdf/tdwaa-2008-sciencepostrpt.pdf on March 6, 2021.

Webb, N. L. (2015a, September). Mathematics DOK definitions. Retrieved at www.webbalign.org/dok-definitions-for-math on August 13, 2021.

Webb, N. L. (2015b, September). Reading DOK definitions. Accessed at www.webbalign.org/dok-definitions-for-reading on August 13, 2021.

Webb, N. L. (2015c, September). "Social studies DOK definitions." Accessed at www.webbalign.org/dok-definitions-for-social-studies on August 13, 2021.

Webb, N. L. (2019, July). DOK Primer. Accessed at www.webbalign.org/dok-primer on August 13, 2021.

Webb, N. L., Alt, M., Ely, R., Cormier, M., & Vesperman, B. (2005, December). *Alignment Report 1: The WEB alignment tool: Development, refinement, and dissemination—Aligning assessment to guide the learning of all students.* Washington, DC: Council of Chief State School Officers. Accessed from https://citeseerx.ist.psu.edu/viewdoc/download?doi=10.1.1.465.7548&rep=rep1&type=pdf on July 10, 2021.

Webb, N. L., & Christopherson, S. (2019, September). *DOK: Categories of cognitive engagement for science.* Accessed at www.webbalign.org/dok-definitions-for-science on August 13, 2021.

Wiggins, G. P., & McTighe, J. (2005). *Understanding by design* (expanded 2nd ed.). Alexandria, VA: Association for Supervision and Curriculum Development.

INDEX

A

affective questions, 145
    for learning targets, 147
Ainsworth, L., 9
alternative names, 13–14
analytical questions, 145
analyzing, 13, 95, 133
Anderson, L. W., 9, 104
The Apprentice, 159, 162–165
argumentative questions, 145
assessments, 49–50, 65
    aligning with standards, 167
    using DOK, 56–57
    using standards to set, 50
authentic learning experiences, 44
author or genre studies, 44

B

Berger, R., 52
Biggs, J., 9
Blackburn, B. R., 70
Blocks, 4–5, 21–25
inquiry-based learning method and model, 142–143
    inverted RTI pyramid and, 70
Bloom, B., 9
Bloom's inverted questioning pyramid, 150
Bloom's Taxonomy, xiii–xiv, 1–2
    revised, 13, 19–21, 25–27, 92–93, 104, 142, 156
Brookhart, S., 118
Buffum, A., 22, 68, 73, 76

C

capstone projects, 44
case studies, 44
Cash, R. M., 62
ceiling of assessment, 29, 143
Chauvin, R., 34
checking phrasing of a learning intentions, 86, 94–97
checks and balances matrix, 112–113
choosing and composing learning targets, 122–124
    chunking and cataloging learning goal targets, 123
    learning goal targets for a multistep procedure or process, 123
    narrowing the instructional purpose, 123–124
chunking, 89, 98
    learning goals separately, 123
    objectives with learning intention, 120
Clapton, E., 64
clarifying context, 86, 89–94
Clark, B., 2
cognitive action verbs, 13–14
cognitive demand
    extended targets that deepen, 128
Cognitive Rigor Questioning (CRQ) Framework, 144
cognitive rigor. *See* rigor
collaboration skills, 40
Common Core State Standards, 2
communication skills, 40
complexity of content knowledge, 10
comprehension, 13
confirming performance expectation, 86–89

Fifty Strategies to Boost Cognitive Engagement
Rebecca Stobaugh

Transform your classroom from one of passive knowledge consumption to one of active engagement. In this well-researched book, Rebecca Stobaugh shares 50 strategies for building a thinking culture that emphasizes essential 21st century skills—from critical thinking and problem solving to teamwork and creativity.
BKF894

Ambitious Instruction
Brad Cawn

Discover a blueprint for making rigor visible, accessible, and actionable in grades 6–12 classrooms. *Ambitious Instruction* guides readers toward using the twin tenets of problem-based learning and synthesis to significantly strengthen students' ability to read, write, and think within and across disciplines.
BKF842

Raising the Rigor
Eileen Depka

This user-friendly resource shares questioning strategies and techniques proven to enhance students' critical thinking skills, deepen their engagement, and better prepare them for college and careers. The author also provides a range of templates, surveys, and checklists for planning instruction, deconstructing academic standards, and increasing classroom rigor.
BKF722

Personalized Deeper Learning
James A. Bellanca

Foster deeper learning with two templates—one for students, the other for teachers—that increase student agency and learning transfer within critical skill sets. Any teacher—regardless of grade, the existing curriculum, or student load—can adapt, scale, and sustain these powerful personalized learning plans.
BKF975

a division of

Solution Tree | Press

Solution Tree

Visit SolutionTree.com or call 800.733.6786 to order.

"Tremendous, tremendous, tremendous!

The speaker made me do some very deep internal reflection about the **PLC process** and the personal responsibility I have in making the school improvement process work **for ALL kids.**"

—Marc Rodriguez, teacher effectiveness coach,
Denver Public Schools, Colorado

PD Services

Our experts draw from decades of research and their own experiences to bring you practical strategies for building and sustaining a high-performing PLC. You can choose from a range of customizable services, from a one-day overview to a multiyear process.

Book your PLC PD today!
888.763.9045

Solution Tree